SERVICE FOR YOUR SOUL

SERVICE FOR YOUR SOUL

Checklist

Introduction 7
Dedication 9
About This Guidebook 11
SECTION 1 - Mode of Transformation: MOT For Your Soul 13
Diagnostic Soul Survey (Part 1) 16
Your Courtesy Light 19
A Little Bit Of Fine Tuning Required 21
Servicing Your Spark Plugs 23
Electrical System – Spiritual Energy 25
Capacities and Limitations 27
Overloaded Vehicle 29
A Spanner in the Works 31
MOT FINDINGS 69
SECTION 2 – Service for your Soul 71
Mind, Soul and Body Check 73
Hot Wheels 77
Gear Shifts 81
Overinflated Tyres 85
The Steering 87
Potholes In Your Road 89
Objects In the Rearview Mirror 95
Beware Of the Hitchhiker 101
The Classic Car Show 107
Eyewitness – Idle Talk 109
The Undercarriage 111
Apply The Handbrake 116
Roadside Assistance 119
DIAGNOSTIC SOUL SURVEY (PART 2) 123
The Higher Power Source 126
The Small Print 128
Connecting Rods 132
About Me 133

Introduction

The idea for this guidebook came from receiving an alert from my garage, reminding me my car was due its MOT and Service.
Not only is an MOT a legal requirement – so definitely important, but it's also the vehicle owner's responsibility to ensure it's roadworthy by getting it booked in and checked out as soon as possible, so you remain on the road safely and legally.
You are more reliant on your car than ever before, and your expectations are much higher.
It could be that you have put all of your trust into the mechanic's knowledge and experience at the garage, and exchanged copious amounts of cash, quietly praying that the vehicle will last that little bit longer.

In a metaphorical sense the maintenance of your human vehicle is just as valid and important as your car parked on your driveway. Ensuring your vehicle is running well and roadworthy, has now taken on a whole new meaning.
How often do you focus on your well-being and energy levels to guarantee you remain dependable and fully functioning?

Dedication

This guidebook is dedicated to my dad, Peter who loved tinkering with his car, was mildly obsessed with anything vehicle related, was an engineer and enjoyed the workings out of anything mechanical. Yet, I believe, due to the lack of tools available at the time, struggled with his mental health that little bit more than he should have had to, lived to the best of his abilities with limited knowledge of his Bi-Polar Disorder diagnosis, struggled to find the peace within and died that bit too soon for me to have got to truly know him.
I wholeheartedly believe that if he'd have been here now, he would have been better understood, accepted for who he was as a Soul, rather than the man his illness portrayed him to be and more equipped to heal from many of the challenges that he experienced.

About This Guidebook

The premise is to provide you with tools and advisories to enable you to fully function and remain on a consistent, positive, high vibrational frequency level. Your Soul is your energetic life force and that to sustain that high vibration and free flowing energy, requires frequent inputs of energetic maintenance.

Think of me as your Soul's, Service Technician, steering you on your spiritual journey. Navigating you around the road map of healing that gently weaves in and out of the following pages. This is a two-fold guide for the Soul, your Soul.

You are a busy, human being and with that in mind, the first section of this guide gives you an opportunity to "lower the dipstick" into the reservoir of your curiosity. The concept is for you to pull over and take a break from the road you have been travelling along since you entered this carriageway of life. For you to travel that little bit deeper into your inner workings. Just like your car that you drive requires an MOT and Service to ensure it is running well, your Soul requires regular check ins to ensure your energy is high and you are traveling trouble free.

It is likely that when you bought your car it came with an owner's manual. Consider this book as being the guide for the safe upkeep of your Soul. It will prepare you for the unexpected, when to operate your hazard lights and other important information to keep your engine running when you find yourself stranded at the side of the road.

The first section; The MOT (Mode of Transformation) takes you through the process of getting to know your Soul, that little bit better. It is not overly complex, there won't be a test and it's not too time consuming. It will, however, give you an insight into the next, more in-depth section. You can put it down and pick it up. Let it gradually permeate and begin to resonate. Then, when you feel you're ready for discovering the nuts and bolts of your Soul and more, you can buckle up and travel that bit further and immerse yourself into Section Two, The Service for Your Soul. It is here where you will be taken on a journey of self-discovery and guidance on how to maintain your vehicle's road worthiness, reliability and overall functionality.

SECTION 1 -
Mode of Transformation: MOT For Your Soul

Spiritual Dimensions

Welcome to your guidebook for your Soul. Here you will find snippets of information that you probably never realised until now, you needed to know. By continuing to read on, you're putting a little bit of your time aside to focus on your Soul. It can be a challenge starting the process of concentrating on parts of you that you may not have considered needed any of your attention, yet as you travel a little deeper into this guidebook, you may find some answers to the subtle questions your Soul has been asking. The answers your Soul needs a little bit of "roadside assistance" with.

As a human, you are an energetic being. To prevent blockages in your energy function – much like a car engine, the energy needs to be able to flow freely within you.

Perhaps you are curious and it may be that you want to know just a little bit more about spiritual energy, what it is that drives you onwards, your true purpose, the part of you that has always been there, the part of you that has been journeying alongside you and within you, yet it's only now that you are paying it some attention. It's only now that you feel is the right time to explore that little bit more. The get up and go within that wants you to keep reading on and proceed that bit further. Kudos to you for listening to your inner driver and giving yourself permission to explore and enter the road that you may have originally thought to be a No Entry, or a No-Go area.

Your Soul is having a quiet word; a whisper, waking you from dawdling in the slow lane. As you continue to read, it may be that you begin to consider that you are not only the skin and bones of the human vehicle you reside in, but you are <u>so</u> much more. You are a magical and powerful Soul living a human experience, and it's now the time to give your Soul your sole attention!

Consider this, are you functioning to your full capacity, or are you are just idling through your human experience?

Diagnostic Soul Survey (Part 1)

"A diagnostic test for a car is to assess the functionality of a vehicle's electronic systems and identify potential issues that could affect it's road worthiness."
A diagnostic Soul survey is to assess how your Soul vehicle is currently running and highlight the areas that may need attention to improve overall performance.

DIAGNOSTIC SYMPTOMS	
1-4 score	
POWER LOSS Lethargic, tired, feeling flat/low.	
VIBRATIONS Get upset easily, feel panicky, physical symptoms, such as lack of sleep.	
OVER-HEATING Regularly losing your temper, snappy, lack of control.	
DIFFICULTY STARTING Your get up and go has got up and gone.	
SLOW ACCELERATION Lack of motivation, sluggish, short bursts of energy but not sustained.	
BRAKES BEHAVING DIFFERENTLY Procrastinating, uninterested in tasks or activities.	
NOISE Sensitive to noise, overstimulated and overwhelmed in busy places.	
SUDDEN ENGINE FAILURE DUE TO WRONG FUEL I have nightmare/terrors. I suffer with indigestion and stomach aches.	
GOOD RUNNING ORDER Overall, you feel like everything is ok.	
FREE OF MECHANICAL PROBLEMS Calm, grounded and even tempered.	
IDLES SMOOTHLY I can sit still easily and am calm. I'm patient and tolerant. I can breathe in and out easily.	
NOT MOVING Sleeping well with no interruptions. No feelings of guilt, remorse or regret.	

The following survey encourages you to take time out of your busy day and really check in on yourself. Use this tool as a means of flagging up any issues you didn't realise you needed assistance with. There are no right or wrong answers and there is no pressure to complete it. It does, however, give you an insight into how your Soul is currently running and highlight some areas that need focussing on.

	NONE OR A LITTLE	SOME OF THE TIME	A GOOD PART OF THE TIME	MOST OF THE TIME
	1	2	3	4

Your Courtesy Light

Underneath your bonnet is a complex system that is running various functions all at different times, yet somehow in smooth, sweet harmony with each other. Synchronising for various purposes and ensuring that you are powering onwards and continuing on your journey relatively trouble free.

Part of the mechanics involved in your vehicle's inner make up is your courtesy light. The life force, that is your Soul. The part of you that shines brightly when fully functioning yet can gradually dim and fade as your door remains open to the more negative experiences, challenges and grief throughout your lifetime.

Be assured that, unlike an actual vehicle, your "courtesy light" only dulls, it cannot go out.

That inner light is your Soul. Your energy within. It might be that your inner light may not be illuminating and brightly shining quite as it once did. Draped in thick layers of dust, grime and debris that it has picked up along life's journey.

Your vehicle works at its best when all its faculties are functioning and running trouble free. Sometimes, however, when one thing begins to struggle, another then may start to sputter and screech or even break down. This guidebook will allow you to step away from your vehicle and look at it from a different angle. From a different perspective and with guidance, you'll be able to begin to understand your vehicle better, the vehicles around you and the reasons your vehicle may behave in such a way that might require some recovery.

Maintaining your vehicle to its full capacity and reliable working order may have been a challenge.

The MOT in this manual will tick off any points of concern you have and allow you the time to focus on your inner light and how to continue to sustain its power.

As a car owner you may put all your trust in an engineer to look at and

diagnose your car troubles. You may not even have considered to check under the bonnet more than a few times, perhaps only to fill up the windscreen washer jets or check on the oil levels.
Much the same with your body, mind, and Soul – you may only be checking in on the very basic check points of maintaining yourself.
Perhaps, like many of us, you haven't considered all of the components that make you who you are, and how some experiences have shaped your journey thus far.
This book is for guidance purposes only and is giving you the permission to begin the process of going as deep as you feel able to, and comfortable with. It may resonate more in certain areas or not at all in others. Yet, it will gradually start the process in buffing up your inner light and slowly begin to fuel your curiosity that has already been prompted to discover more.
Your Soul has given you a minor collision within. Encouraging you to put the handbrake on and focus on the unique mode of transport you are moving along in.
Your vehicle is powered by forces of energy that you may not have even contemplated, until now. For this energy to flow freely and without the potential to break down, you need consistent levels of frequency to maintain a healthy, well balanced, safe and roadworthy, mode of transport.
To maintain harmonious engagement with others, your Soul needs frequent checks on its general well-being and running of functions.

Your Soul has a purpose here, one that is to grow and evolve, and yes, as with any experiences, your vehicle will pick up some miles on the clock, nasty bumps and scratches along the way, it's how you deal with the situations of life, rather than the situations themselves that is key. This will give energy the opportunity to flow faster, and your inner light won't be so dimmed for quite so long. Therefore, however tarnished your light is at this moment, it's only on that setting for a short while. Energy can move in periods of smooth driving but there will also be moments of stop – start traffic. You may feel stuck, stagnant or unable to see the light at the end of the tunnel, but trust that it's there and that you have the power within to turn that switch back up to full brightness.

Equally, by remembering your true worth, you mustn't feel that you should dim your light so often that all your fuel is syphoned out of you. By maintaining a steady flow of energy, and keeping your interior light shining, try to embrace the company of those on your team. The ones who genuinely want the best for you, those who support and encourage you, those who genuinely believe in you and ignite those passions within.

A Little Bit Of Fine Tuning Required

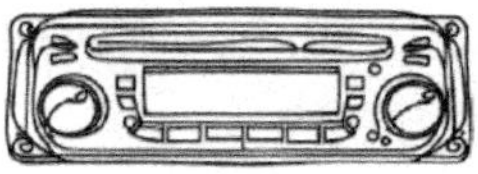

Right, this is where you need to shift up a gear and crank up the volume of your inner car stereo -get those speakers pulsating as this is the important stuff! Think of a radio station. You already know that the frequency that plays upbeat, happy songs is going to make you feel differently from the station that is based on just talking, discussing politics or world news. For a variety of reasons, you may have been "tuned into" the wrong radio channel, the "wrong frequency" for your Soul's needs and requirements, and it may have caused you more bumps in the road than you think you should have had, and possibly some depression along the way. To retune will take courage, determination and persistence, but I suggest the more listening figures for this particular station the better!

By re-tuning and finding the sweet spot of the more upbeat, higher frequency - you can already feel your energy begin to rise.

By ensuring that your stereo speakers are balanced, will minimise any interference and cancel out the negative signal. Think of tuning into the higher radio frequency with the volume at maximum, the windows open, and the wind blowing through your hair. You'll feel the difference in energy output and vibration straight away. By doing this, others will feel your energy frequency change too. They will either come with you for the ride and join you on your high vibe road trip or take off on a side road to follow a slightly different carriageway.

Maintaining that frequency, will align your body, mind and Soul and begin to take away any anxieties and concerns. It will assist in providing you with a less fear-based life and a much more positive; "what will be will be" type of existence. Less overthinking and more free thinking.

Advisory

You probably can tell if you are vibrating on higher or lower levels by being in tune with how you feel, observing others around you and any environmental factors and situations.

A higher vibrational frequency creates the happy atmosphere; one that is light, bright and free flowing. A lower vibrational frequency is when the atmosphere could be cut with a knife, making you feel uncomfortable and unbalanced.

By maintaining a higher frequency and balancing the speakers, you will not only make your journey here energetically freer, but you will also allow the gateway to your Soul, and beyond to open up that bit easier too.

Servicing Your Spark Plugs

When you had a few less miles on your clock, do you remember that feeling of giddy excitement bubbling within? Just like when the windscreen washer jet fizzes, and pops, vibrating through your whole being. It might have been a Christmas Eve - anticipating your requested gift from Father Christmas or the last day of school before the summer holidays. Imagining the weeks of school free days that lay ahead. There was a fun, relaxed atmosphere and the best bit was that you didn't have to do any schoolwork that day either. You may have brought in your favourite board game, and you knew that would be the only thing that you had to put your mind to. Maybe you got those sparky feelings when you were about to set off on a family holiday- imagining sandcastles and fish and chips on the beach or welcoming a new sibling or pet into the family. You may have got excited about a new family car, a new house and a bedroom all to yourself or having free reign in a toy shop. Friends coming to tea or to sleep over. Playing out until you got called in for bedtime, losing yourself in your imagination and creating stories and characters for your toys. Listening to the chart rundown and heading to the record shop to send it to number one. Moments of sheer abandon and fun, with none of the worries it seemed that the "grown-ups" had to deal with.

If you could bottle those exciting times and vibrations from when you were a child, soak them up, and create the same bubbly energy felt or experienced then - now - wow! You will be popping and banging, fizzing and whizzing - existing on a lovely high vibrational frequency.

Take this moment to contemplate a situation in your past that made you feel

elevated, exhilarated, and electrified. Now sit with that feeling.
Let it fill up your internal fuel tank, as it travels up and down your vehicle in waves. Be a grown-up child. Consider your responsibilities as imaginative play on a daily basis. A different mindset is all that is required.
To feel good inside, means you are tuned into a high vibrational frequency. The vibrational frequency you were always meant to experience. To feel joy is not just for childhood. It's for life. It elevates and powers you onwards.
As you grew up and experienced the bends and forks in the road of reaching adulthood, you probably unconsciously adjusted away from a "childlike" vibrational way of being, as society deemed it no longer how you were supposed to be. Or maybe you still yearned for that high vibrational existence associated with childhood but found it out of your reach. Society encourages you to believe that you should act and behave in a certain way. One that doesn't draw unnecessary attention to you and one that matches your age, to act with maturity and to focus on the intense, seriousness of life. It's now time to give yourself the permission to feel the joy and happiness, you were always meant to experience.

Electrical System – Spiritual Energy

"Most electrical parts accept the current flowing to and from them in only one direction. Most components in the ancillary circuit are wired through the ignition switch, so they only work when the key is turned."

When in the company of someone or a group of people who align with your energetic vibration, you will feel at ease, calm, accepted, free and the flow between you is easy, non-threatening. There are no awkward silences, icky feelings or communication barriers. Instead, there is laughter, lightness, fun and a feeling of "coming home". These Souls are on your vibrational wavelength and replenish your energy on a subtle level. Those that drain your energy are not on your vibrational frequency. Unknowingly, these people can cause you to feel drained, emotionally exhausted, and in need of recharging. The difficulty is that we don't know until we are in the presence of all vibrations.
Every day you will exchange energy. Whether it's the postman or the cat, your partner or a passer- by; energy is being exchanged.

Advisory

The energy exchanged is going to be positive and negative. As you've now started to understand our energy relates to that of all other living beings, be they animals or plants. This is because it is a subtle vibrational means of connecting to all living things. It has no language, it is an energetic connection that you may not be consciously aware of, yet its only restrictions are if it gets blocked, supressed or drained.

When travelling along life's long and winding road, consider all the various lanes that are all heading in the same direction. Your Soul will come into contact with these energies every day. You may want to consider which lane you are currently travelling in too.

- There'll be some who are driving along in their automatic cars on the inside lane at a steady pace and within the speed limits. Travelling along with the visor down and in "D" gear.
- There'll be those in the middle lane of life, in their manual vehicles who are heading for their destination with visor up, in top gear and often at a faster pace who overtake those on the inside lane, but don't necessarily get there any quicker, just seem to move along with that bit more momentum.
- Then there are those in the fast lane. These Souls seem to be on a mission both in life and action, they may zoom along, over taking everyone in their path both metaphorically and subjectively. They may be the ones who also leave their mark and leave the highway sooner than anticipated, or they're the vehicles that end up closing a lane causing a tailback or are the ones on the hard shoulder with smoke escaping from under their bonnets!

Capacities and Limitations

You've felt it, that sensation of running on empty. Living off fumes and barely functioning. When this happens, you may feel unbalanced, depressed, anxious, lethargic, unable to complete simple tasks, and limited in how you can conduct a healthy, balanced and enjoyable existence. The road ahead can often appear to be littered with obstacles and alternative routes. When your fuel is depleted, those obstacles come towards you thick and fast and you're unable to manoeuvre around them sufficiently. This can cause your Soul to tire, your courtesy light to dim, and your engine to even break down.

I know when my energy is running low, that if there was an unexpected hazard, I wouldn't be prepared and able to function effectively. This can really take its toll on me and others around me. I become impatient, short tempered, exhausted, unbalanced and overwhelmed. Those around me are caught in the headlights and struggle too in how to drive through my red mist.

As you progress through this guidebook, you'll get hints designed to provide you with roadside technical assistance and support for your ongoing journey and that of healing your Soul. When "healing" is mentioned, the purpose behind it is for you to consider on an intentional level all of what you have experienced so far in your lifetime. Why components of life can often trigger a negative reaction, and how the process of healing will start high vibrational energy to flow freely through you, therefore reaching the level of frequency we are aiming to maintain. This will give you guidance and permission to begin your journey fully functioning and reaching optimum capacity. The highway is endless, with no limitations when you are truly firing on all cylinders.

Notes and Observations

Overloaded Vehicle

Think of a time where you have experienced an all-consuming feeling that you can't fully comprehend. Where you seem to have taken on the world's troubles as well as your own. A feeling that you've lost yourself completely and feel extremely overwhelmed. The energy or feeling that you carry during this could be comparable to being stuck in a very tight parking spot, or that 3-point turn of relief has suddenly developed into a complex manoeuvre, plus a minor scrape that you hope no one had noticed!

The wider world is a mighty big place. It would be quite a responsibility to keep that in check as well as yourself.

A low, but very affecting energetic frequency is that of fear. If over exposed to this frequency through scare mongering, excessive scrolling on social media and world news you can start to take on the fear that the stories are in some way going to happen to you or a loved one. You take on the fear of another's reality. You are connected to all other living beings, but you can't truly live the life of others. You can only live your life and the reality you choose to create.

Advisory

Ensure that you are regularly checking in on the maintenance of your Soul and boosting your energy levels, prioritising your needs and requirements and considering how you react and respond to situations, you will then energetically send a high vibrational, healing frequency out into the wider world. Out to the collective. The world will hold your light, and powerful, positive energy and power on.

When you are constantly "doing", as well as becoming physically tired, your Soul gets exhausted too. You are a human being, not a human doing. Due to old, low vibrational societal conditioning, you may believe that doing is a good thing and seemingly not doing something is wrong, and equates to laziness, selfishness and "not contributing to society."

However, doing nothing is just as vital as doing something. It's balancing the two activities that can be the challenge. For a vehicle to be balanced the car's mass, centre of gravity, wheelbase, suspension, tyres, steering and aerodynamics need to be fully functioning to provide stability. Much the same as humans, you need to have a stable level of balance to ensure you don't burnout, breakdown or limit your full potential. Symptoms of a vehicle's balance shaft degrading is stalling, misfiring and rough idling. Just like when there is too much stress, when there isn't any, our nervous systems react with opposite symptoms. So, from feeling overwhelmed and panicky when experiencing too much stress and stimulation, when not experiencing enough, you may also experience panicky symptoms infused with a lack of energy, making you feel sluggish, and lacking in the powerful motivation that as a human you need a plentiful balance of.

On a personal note, I experienced panic attacks when I was stuck in a loop that I didn't think I could leave. I was doing a rather mundane job that had reached the point of me being able to do it with my eyes closed. I felt alone, unappreciated and I took no pleasure in doing it anymore. In hindsight my Soul was working through my nervous system, which responded by causing my engine to misfire just enough for me to notice and to try to find a solution to preventing more moments of overwhelm and investigating into why I was unbalanced and not firing on all my cylinders.

Your unique vehicle requires equal measures of stimulation and calm. When this is achieved your equilibrium is in a state of balance physically and mindfully.

Once you have a bit more of an understanding of how your human system functions it can give you the permission your Soul craves to draw a line in the sand. Park up. Start the engine over again and continue your journey in a less unbalanced way.

A Spanner in the Works

Let's jack this up!

Energy needs the opportunities to move and to shift. When you feel like you are experiencing a heaviness within, and it feels like old, stagnant, gloop, this is an indication that your Soul requires a boost energetically. Your Soul is calling out for a mood uplift, to energize and to recharge.

Following, are 14 advisories to push that old energy away. Look upon this as your full oil change.

Notes and Observations

1. SHOCK ABSORBERS: AFFIRMATIONS

Affirmations are words and phrases that are short and to the point. By verbalising them out loud or in your head, you are affirming your intent. The more you say them by creating a habit, your subconscious part of your brain will gradually take the intentional positive words quite literally and your Soul will begin purring like a kitten as it soaks up the high vibrational, joyous, happy and affirming messages, just like a sponge at the car wash! You will begin to feel lighter, brighter and have more of a sense of continual movement. You will see your world just that little bit more in colour, with the full beams brightly guiding your way. I encourage you to continue these affirmations beyond 30 days as then a habit will form.

Say these affirmations out loud, daily in the morning to start the day in a positive way. It may take a bit of practice, and you may feel a little uncomfortable to begin with yet saying them out loud shifts your mindset. Focusing your tone of voice with true intention will power up your inner workings considerably.

BEAT THE RUSH HOUR AFFIRMATIONS:

"I am abundant."
"I am worthy."
"I am successful."
"I am financially stable."
"I am creating a lifestyle that I love."
"I am more than enough."
"I am worthy of overwhelming success."
"I feel calm and confident of my actions behind the wheel."

Try these next affirmations throughout the day. If there are people about, and you feel awkward then say these ones in your head but with just the same, positive intention:

FULLY CHARGED ENERGY AFFIRMATIONS:

"Even if I take a wrong turn, I am exactly where I am meant to be."
"Every day is an opportunity to grow and learn."
"I am willing to learn through love."
"I am on the right road."
"I am aligned with the universe."
"I'm a magnet for miracles."
"My true power lies in this present moment."
"I am a Soul having a human experience."

The following affirmations are powerful too and best to say as you retire after your day. By expressing your gratitude, you are not taking your abundance for granted and you are grateful for all the positives in your life:

HIGH HORSEPOWER Gratitude Affirmations:

"I am grateful for the blessings in my life, both big and small."
"I am grateful to be, and to accept myself."
"I am grateful for all the experiences I've had in my life so far."
"I am grateful for my freedom."
"I am grateful to be part of this amazing universe."
"I am grateful for the beauty of the nature that's all around me."
"I am grateful to feel a spectrum of amazing emotions."
"My drive to live life to the fullest, gets stronger day by day."

You can choose the affirmations that resonate the most and mix and match if you prefer; taking two from each group may work better for you and your current circumstances.

The main advisory from regular affirmations is for them not to feel like a chore, which will deplete your energy levels.

The high energy that the positive words and affirmations hold, will boost your Soul and are good, happy and uplifting energetic vibrations. Therefore, speaking these affirmations will raise your energy frequency. You know how it feels internally to be bombarded with criticism or negative language and how deflated and energetically low it leaves you. This is because your mini universe within -the subconscious part of your human brain, cannot differentiate between what is language and its meaning, and will take whatever words are spoken as truth as it responds to the tone and authentic intention. It has no concept of whether it's right or wrong, black or white, up or down or whether something is positive or negative, unless the vibration is high. This is then put out into your world on a large scale and your reality starts to be manufactured. Therefore, the higher the energy frequency, your positive narrative, tone and intention – though subtle, can be "felt" and understood on a Soul level. Imagine putting the wrong fuel into your car. It may run for a short distance but soon begin to slow down and finally come to a standstill. It has been fed inappropriate means of functioning and is now unable to run at all. Your Soul responds to positive words and affirmations to maintain high energy levels, counteract depression, suppression and "dis - ease." Affirmations help your Soul to function better and run trouble free.

Notes and Observations

2. DON'T DEPRECIATE – APPRECIATE!!

How often do you go through your day focusing on all the negative situations and experiences you have had, rather than all the positive moments? The more energy you put into concentrating on, and sharing the negatives, embarrassing situations or awkward times in the day, the more you are cementing negativity and lowering your positive energetic frequency. You are adding an emotion to the story. Instead, focus on all the good things that have occurred; however small they may seem to be, and practice gratitude for those little wins. By doing this, you are channelling positive energy from your inner mini universe out into the collective universe and creating a higher frequency.

Focus on positive words and intent. Fuel your Soul with appreciation for your whole existence. For example:

"I am grateful that I woke up to the most beautiful sunrise this morning, and really appreciated the warm, golden glow as the day began to awaken too."

"I am grateful to be able to walk to work this morning and appreciate my good health."

The more gratitude and appreciation you put out into the collective universe, you will notice an energetic shift and your energy rising from your feet to the crown of your head. You'll notice more in your surroundings and feel less comfortable complaining about someone or something if you continue this practice.

Gratitude comes straight from your heart space, and this has no judgement, criticism or chastisement or hate. It's full of joy, love, acceptance and abundance. If you don't feel gratitude, then you may be trapped in your "headspace". The part of you that has been conditioned to react and respond in a certain way. As time goes on, you will certainly be able to differentiate between the two, your headspace and your heart space

On a greater scale, the collective universe is a life-force source of all energy – constantly "listening" to your inner thoughts, and outer words, which are heard and accepted on a frequency level. The universe has "heard" you, and if you have negative frequency, will accept that as the way in which you wish to project.

If at this point, you've reached a situation where you feel that the whole world is against you, it's because the more negative thoughts and feelings you have, the more negative the overall experiences you will have. This then reaffirms what you believe to be true, and you have created this as your reality. Therefore, more potholes and troubles arise in the road ahead. This is because what you are projecting outwardly is a low vibrational frequency. Language, or words used are not how the universe interprets your thoughts and emotions, instead it works with energetic frequency that are attached to those thoughts and intentions. If lots of people have the same negative thoughts and are putting them out into the universe, you can imagine what is happening on a more global scale. Hence why igniting your passions, your love, your joy in your current existence will spread throughout and create great change that will have a positive effect not just on you but those around you too.

Advisory

Try this short Gratitude Meditation - may be record it on your phone and listen to it as you fall asleep with some pleasant music playing in the background. DO NOT LISTEN TO THIS WHILE DRIVING.

As I fill up my energetic fuel tank with light, love, and positive thoughts of gratitude -

I affirm my appreciation of my health, my peace, my happiness, my abundance and the free- flowing road that lies ahead of me.

I am grateful for all that I have been given from the road less travelled by my ancestors.

I am grateful for the abundance and joy that awaits me on my future journey.

I visualise a harmonious, healthy, healing energy lighting the way, enveloping me in its power and accepting me of my true self.

As my fuel tank overflows with healing, positive energy, I embody my gratitude and carry a glowing light that shines far and wide, forever and always.

3. A JOURNEY INTO JOURNALING:

Just like pressing the cruise control button on your car and allowing it to travel at an uninterrupted, steady speed; journaling provides the same, effortless, relief from the day-to-day stuff that you experience – but may not have had time to acknowledge, decompress from and process.
Journaling is not the same as having a diary and entering your appointments, where you went and what you did. Journaling is so much more than that and will provide you with solace, comfort and insight. It is Soul led and as you journal more, your Soul will begin to take over the narrative in a powerful, positive way – if you let it!

Advisory

Firstly, make the whole process a journey of personal discovery. By making this a special moment for you and your Soul, it will allow the words to flow, the experience to be pleasurable and the overall outcome, to be positive.

A new notebook and pen with enthused energy will allow you to focus on the process of writing down your inner highest thoughts. Your Soul has been gently nudging you for a while now and although there are many ways in which your Soul can communicate with you – through signs, lyrics in music and experiences - putting pen to paper allows your Soul to have free reign and be able to fully express its wants and desires.
Effective journalling can capture your true inner thoughts and your Soul's advisories that perhaps you don't ordinarily hear, or choose to ignore, even though the messages may be quite prominent and flashing at you with some intensity!

Be prepared for it all to flow out from you once you get started, the good, the bad and everything in between!

To journal is to release, to inspire, to consider, to aspire and to realise rather than holding on to everything in your head, creating a scrapyard of burnt-out vehicles; writing it all down and reading it back to yourself gives you a whole new perspective, power and concept of everything. You can even save it for that slow day and look back to see the progress made so far on your spiritual journey.

And I mean everything. By creating an output for your inner most thoughts, you are shedding some of the old energy that isn't serving you. You are now beginning to turn your energy vibration up, and learning to accept all the many dimensions, flaws and sides that you have within, and maybe hide from the outside world. This will aid in the process of accepting yourself; scuffs, scratches and all.

BLIND SPOT:

If you are not a comfortable writer and don't feel that pull to express your inner conversations on paper, then you may find it just as useful to record your entry on your phone or whichever device best suits.

Journaling is a means of expression, yet there is a definite difference in the experience. For example, the more you do it, the more you will realise the change that begins as you connect with your Soul. You will be able to tell the difference between your head's thoughts and your Soul speaking through you. It's like having a mini-Soul engineer inside. Your Soul loves you unconditionally and will begin to seep through the pages encouraging you to believe in yourself and praising your achievements up to this point. There's nothing better for switching up the vibration and raising the bar. Your Soul will also forgive your actions and, of course, forgiveness has such a strong emotional connection with you and your mental health and general well-being. After your journal entry you'll feel lighter, inspired and less heavy and not so weighed down with negative thoughts and feelings.

Advisory

HOW TO JOURNAL EFFECTIVELY:

Commit to a daily journal entry if possible. The length of what you write isn't important, but the overall commitment to yourself and your Soul, begins to open the belief system that your well-being is important and purposeful.

Organise the environment you plan to journal in. Keep it cool and private. Maybe some inspiring music on in the background, light candles/incense and keep refreshed.

Try not to be disturbed or distracted as this will interrupt the flow and inner conversations. Switch off the mobile phone and laptop, (unless that's what you're journalling on), and embrace the disconnection of the conscious world, and the connection with your Soul. Write down all of your thoughts and look for the truth beyond and beneath the surface of noise.

You're going on an unplanned road trip with your Soul, and like any unplanned trip, you start not really knowing where you're heading, but as the journey progresses you get to see all the things you never imagined, enjoy new experiences, the twists and turns of the unknown road ahead will give you a deep connection with the protagonist of this guidebook!!

It might be that what you write down makes no sense to anyone else but yourself. It may be pictures, graphics, spider charts, doodles, all sorts of means of expression that begins to untangle some of the pressures of every day.

Be prepared for some tears during the process, especially at the beginning. I encourage you to let the tears flow and embrace the release of any built-up pressures and pain.

You will know when you are writing from your Soul as you won't have the mental strength to argue or disagree with what is coming through you. It just is, and you accept it.

Journal to ask advice. Journal to align with your Soul. Journal to find energetic vibrations. Journal to find solution and peace within. Store your writings where they are accessible for your eyes only. Remember that peace within, means peace for all those who are connected to you and all those in the much wider world.

Some journal prompts to rev up your creativity and prompt a conversation with your Soul:

1. Where would your ideal magical road trip be to and why, and who might come along for the ride?
2. If you could only ever listen to one genre of music for the rest of your life, what might it be?
3. If your life were a book, how would a new chapter start?
4. The time travelling campervan that can take you forward and back in time to future tech and historical events.
5. What would your mode of transportation be on your ideal road trip – no restrictions?
6. Who would be your ideal Thelma to your Louise while cruising down the highway?
7. If you could choose your perfect destination to settle, where would it be and why there?

4. A BIT OF "OFFROADING"

Getting out and about in nature is a source of continuous joy. Try not to immediately think that you haven't got the time, or that you have other things to do that you wish to prioritise over experiencing a free, healthy, and life-balancing activity. Around every corner is a green space and if you seek it, you will find it!

A simple wander in the woods, a jog in the park or a run, away from the roadside, will recharge your energy levels within minutes and stimulate your all too often forgotten senses.

Motion moves any stagnant energy that might be lingering and preventing you from continuing your journey with joy and ease. It can be quite overwhelming experiencing all the busyness and low vibrational frequency that can often surround you. As an energetic being, "escaping" from that will provide just enough of the required stimuli for your senses to manage and therefore begin your Soul's recharging process. Just like your mobile needs charging from constant usage at the end of the day, so does your Soul.

Advisory

When you next take a walk in the woods for example, really appreciate your surroundings in a mindful way. Mindfulness is being fully aware of your environment and embracing the here and now. Your natural mode may well be to keep moving forward yet being distracted by the deadline, problem or issue. By using your senses, you can begin to immerse in the natural energies surrounding you and escape. Fill up your senses. Enjoy the sights and smells. Feel the sensation of the tree roots beneath your feet. Soak up your surroundings and sense the rhythm of this environment, the birdsong and the natural order of things under the canopy of the living, breathing trees.

Don't forget to always look up. Often, we forget to look up at the sky, or beyond the trees. The shapes of the branches or the cloud formation, all give you something different to focus on, which will stop any chatter in your mind and calm your overworked senses. It won't take long before you begin to feel lighter within, recharged and topped up with natural energy and not depleted.

You could give your walk a purpose too. Have a camera or your phone with you and take themed pictures. Be it birds, trees, landscapes or specifically colours of things that you see, like yellow daffodils, green meadow banks or blue skies. These activities are focusing your mind on alternatives rather than stress and anxious thoughts, therefore allowing you to decompress and unwind. To calm and recharge your energy levels.

5. PUMP UP THE VOLUME!!

Let's shift that stagnant, negative energy and move to the music! Music is such an emotive yet personal modality and uniquely yours to dance, sing, jump around or head bang to. Wind those windows down to immerse in all that it gives you. Memories that make you happy. A tune that transports you back to a time when you were less troubled and free-thinking, an emotive and stirring composition or a song where the lyrics just resonate and make you feel that it was written with you in mind.

Crank up the volume. Stick some headphones on to fully immerse yourself and just dance as if you're the only person in the room.

Make a mental note of how you feel before and after and how free you energetically feel during the experience.

Tune into its rhythm and beat, tap your feet, the steering wheel, shake a tambourine or create a pan lid drum – whatever you feel the urge to do!

Get your fists pumping, and embrace the musical mindset magic this experience will motivate for your Soul.

For a more profound musical experience, release pent up emotions and listen to a song that doesn't fail to give you the feels. You know the one! You can still move and sway to the intoxicating melody and allow it to wash over you as well as wash away any negative emotions. Keep that energy in motion.

Here are a few songs that will get you moving and drive along to:

- SURVIVOR: EYE OF THE TIGER
- MEATLOAF: PARADISE BY THE DASHBOARD LIGHT
- WILSON PICKETT: MUSTANG SALLY
- FRANKIE VALLI AND THE FOUR SEASONS: THE NIGHT
- ARTHUR CONLEY – SWEET SOUL MUSIC
- CHUCK BERRY: NO PARTICULAR PLACE TO GO
- GARY NUMAN: CARS
- BRUCE SPRINGSTEEN: BORN TO RUN
- SHANIA TWAIN: IN MY CAR (I'LL BE THE DRIVER)
- RIHANNA: SHUT UP AND DRIVE
- ROY ORBISON: I DROVE ALL NIGHT
- CANNED HEAT: ON THE ROAD AGAIN
- ACDC: HIGHWAY TO HELL
- BILLY OCEAN: GET OUTTA MY DREAMS, AND INTO MY CAR
- MADNESS: DRIVING IN MY CAR

Some tunes that will move your emotions and give you those "feels":

- ANDREA BOCELLI: ALI DI LIBARATA
- ENNIO MORRICONE, YO-YO-MA, ROMA SINFONIETTA: LADY CALIPH: DINNER
- BEETHOVEN: SYMPHONY NUMBER 7 IN A MAJOR
- PETER GABRIEL AND KATE BUSH: DON'T GIVE UP
- MASSIVE ATTACK: BE THANKFUL FOR WHAT YOU'VE GOT
- ROBERT HAIG COXON: COMING HOME
- EVA CASSIDY: YOU TAKE MY BREATH AWAY
- ERIC CLAPTON: TEARS IN HEAVEN
- R.E.M: EVERYBODY HURTS
- THE CARS: DRIVE
- SNOW PATROL: CHASING CARS
- QUEEN: LOVE OF MY LIFE
- NICK DRAKE: NORTHERN SKY

6. PRESSURE WASH THAT PRESSURE OFF!

As a spiritual being, protected by your human bodywork, going through your day-to-day routine from getting up in the morning to returning to your bed at night, means that you have unwittingly been exposed to a lot of people and a lot of their various energies.

When your car needs a good clean you will see all the dust, the mud sprays and the mucky sills that are crying out for a good soapy sponge to clean away the debris and residual grime it has accumulated throughout the days and weeks. Just like heading to the carwash to scrub away all the muck you've collected on your travels, a shower or bath will not only clean away the physical dirt, but it will cleanse you on an energetic level as well. Rather than seeing the residual energy left on you by others, you will be able to feel it instead. It may be that you've never considered the reasons you may feel tired and drained, more impatient and crochety. Contemplate that although you cannot see it in a visual sense it doesn't mean it isn't happening and doesn't exist.

To prevent causing unnecessary distress for yourself and those in your vicinity, getting yourself under the shower and visualising all the negativity that may have latched on to you from your day is a powerful solution. Watching it as it drains away in the flow of the water, will certainly make you sense the improvement in your overall function. Like a magnet, allow the water to soak up negativity and provide a whole new shiny vehicle underneath that is raring to go, full of fresh ideas and aspirations. Having a relaxing soak will have the same effect and as you concentrate on washing off the day's murky bits, imagine the water as a cleansing, energetic source that not only is cleaning your body but is cleansing your mind and Soul too. You are 60% water after all, so if you soak up the energies on the inside, imagine the power of the water on the outside!

Have a shower at different times in the day as well. This shifts excess negative energy that you'd possibly normally carry for most of the day. Visualise all your woes and those of others, spiral down the drain and afterwards, feel invigorated, refreshed and revitalized so when you leave your bathroom you are like a pristine, showroom specimen! (Fluffy, warm towels are a must too!!)

Notes and Observations

7. DIP YOUR HEADLIGHTS

Your vehicle requires the balance of both physical tiredness and a settled, quiet mind. However, achieving that balance may prove challenging.

There's a natural rhythm to your sleep pattern. Your whole vehicle is wired up to experience various depths and stages to warrant a restorative night's sleep. If one or more of these stages is interrupted, then the opportunity of maintaining the balance starts to diminish. If you've gone without your full quota – that is unique to you - then you'll certainly be aware of how it can affect your well-being.

Sleep is a fantastic opportunity for your subconscious as it gets to sort out and organise the day you've just experienced, in a visual and symbolic way when dreaming. There's renewing and repairing your bodywork, and right under the bonnet, there's a chance for your Soul to go on a little trip, free from the human restrictions. All this is happening between 6-12 hours of your life!

A good, refreshing sleep will set you up for the day and power your through until you return to start the pattern again. That is why it is important to try to maintain a routine that suits your needs and requirements.

Advisory

ADVISORIES ON COMBATTING SLEEP DIFFICULTIES:

- Create a wind down routine that works for you, at least an hour before bed. Your subconscious loves order and routine.
- Don't watch or listen to the news or overly violence led films or documentaries during your wind down period.
- Try not to consume stimulants right before bedtime, such as coffee.
- Alcohol; while it may feel relaxing and make you drowsy can reduce sleep quality so best to avoid when you want to be sure of getting replenishing sleep.
- Write in a bedtime journal. This will give you time to reduce intrusive thoughts, if you use this time to sort through any worries and concerns
- Read a book that is interesting, though not too stimulating. You might want to listen to a guided mediation or some classical music.
- Turn off your Wi-Fi and Blue Tooth.
- Don't charge your device too close to your head, i.e. not next to you on the bedside table.
- Blue light interrupts and disturbs your natural rhythm. Avoid mobile phone use when it is dark, and or through the night if you wake up.
- Use black out blinds, dark curtains or an eye mask to ensure total darkness
- Regulate the temperature of the room and the bedding. Ensuring you aren't too hot or too cold. Open a window for some fresh, free flowing air or use a fan.
- Use ear plugs to reduce noise interruptions such as snoring or birdsong.
- Try not to chastise yourself or get frustrated if you don't get a good night's sleep. Instead, use this as a means of self-discovery. Could it be that there's an area in your life that you aren't aligned with? The energy feels inauthentic and forced and that may be causing you concern and worry? Are you feeling something in your Soul? Use this disturbance as a guide in looking into finding out the root cause of what might be imposing on your rest.

8. CLEAN YOUR SPACE – INTERIOR VALET

Have you ever considered that a messy and cluttered environment can create a messy and cluttered energy frequency?

Think of all the dust that accumulates around your handbrake, the leftovers in the glove compartment or the leaves and twigs in the footwell of your vehicle. It is just the same with your energy. If you work in a messy space, you will create a dense and heavy energy that you transmute to. A much lighter frequency is one that is fresh, clean, uncluttered, and organised.

You might not have considered that your environment around you, is an extension of you. If your work environment, home or interior of your car is overwhelmed with heavy, dusty, dirty, oily, mess and you quite literally cannot see your way through the piles of papers, rubbish and waste that have accumulated – then you can only envisage the challenges it would be for your free-flowing energy to be able to flow freely!

What is your current environment like? Be it at home, at work or the footwell of your car; is there anything that you could improve or change?

This may take some doing. Not just physically, but on many other levels too. For example, if you have been so used to "pulling your sun visor down" on your surroundings and perhaps accepting that this is how you prefer to live, because that is what you are used to – it may take a little work on your part to begin the process of clearing out and creating a tidier space. Be reassured though, that as you go through the process of tidying and cleaning up after yourself, the energy will gradually lift and begin to cascade around you. You will then be emitting a higher vibration of energy out into your environment – your world.

Visualise the sensations of the "feels" of collecting a newly valeted car that is just like new and pristine and all those annoying smeared, faded bits are now polished. A shiny dashboard, fresh upholstery and a gleaming interior is how you need to compare your energy through life - that's the level of frequency that you are aiming for.

Notes and Observations

9.THE CORRECT FUEL FOR OPTIMUM PERFORMANCE: VEHICLE BODY AND STRUCTURE

You know that the correct fuel and oil for your car will make it run well and any kind of journey you take should proceed trouble free.
However, if you didn't put in the correct fuel, or engine oil, your car probably wouldn't get very far before running into trouble. Much the same as you feel if you've overdone it in the food and drinks your body just isn't designed for.
The best fuel to consume is a diet high in fresh, plant-based, unprocessed, raw produce. All that is jampacked with healthy, balanced goodies. Fruit and vegetables are grown from the earth from nuts and seeds. With that in mind, the energy of the earth has naturally infused the fresh fruit and vegetables with high frequency energy and your body will only thank you for giving it a healthy and nutritionally balanced diet to create a high vibration.
Consider the more processed food that you consume against the fresher options and compare how they make you feel. Using dirty fuel could cause defective and faulty engine start-ups and performance. It may mean stalling and misfiring and creating some part failures too!
Like going to a reputable garage rather than a back street one for your fuel, your Soul will thank you for a sediment free fuel source in the long run.
It's also about getting the balance right. Your relationship with food on a Soul level may not have been something that you have ever considered. But if you have moments of guilt and regret, that lowers the vibrational frequency.
Consider these questions below and honestly answer them to the best of your ability.

How have you felt after too much of the fuel your body wasn't designed for?

In what way does it affect your general well-being? Do your emotions come to the fore?

Do you feel guilty, upset, disappointed or depressed when choosing to eat more processed food?

Do you consume more alcohol to enhance your experience or to block out pain?

Do you feel blocked, unfocused, spaced out or shaky after too much sugar or caffeine for example?

From a vibrational point of view, if your energy is depleted and the cause is due to topping up with the wrong fuel, then gradually introduce the fresh foods that are available and water rather than fizzy, highly caffeinated, sugary drinks for a few days and watch how you energetically rise and generally feel lighter, fresher and healthier. Anything that looks bright, artificial and shiny has probably been tampered with, so probably best to drive on to the next forecourt along for fresher options.

YOUR DIET IS NOT JUST WHAT YOU EAT. IT'S WHAT YOU WATCH, WHAT YOU LISTEN TO, WHAT YOU READ, THE PEOPLE YOU ASSOCIATE WITH....BE MINDFUL OF THE THINGS YOU PUT INTO YOUR BODY EMOTIONALLY, SPIRITUALLY AND PHYSICALLY.

So here you are navigating your way through life and most advisories given so far in this guidebook are for you to pay attention to not only your Soul but the vehicle that you reside in.
Raising the vibe of your fuel can happen during preparation and passing your own vibration on to what you are preparing. Think happy and positive thoughts while cooking and transfer your high vibe frequency to the meals you prepare.

Advisory

Here's some high vibe fuels to consume for optimum performance:

- Fresh vegetables and legumes.
- Fresh herbs.
- Fresh fruits.
- Sprouts, shoots and microgreens.
- Natural organic spices.
- Fermented foods for your gut health.
- Raw nuts and seeds.
- Raw honey.
- Sustainly caught fish.
- High quality dairy and meat products.

Here's a list of low performance, dirty fuel to avoid:

- Genetically modified.
- Highly processed.
- Synthetic, artificial additives.
- Processed flours.
- Artificial sugars and sweeteners.
- Deep fried.
- Snacks with sugar and flavourings.
- Caffeine in large amounts.
- Farmed fish and improperly raised animals.

"MOVEMENT THAT INSPIRES AND CREATES PASSION FOR LIFE…."

- **RUNNING – BENEFITS:** Grounding, energy boosting, increases confidence and stamina.
- **CYCLING – BENEFITS:** Empowerment, heart health and emotional balance.
- **KAYAKING – BENEFITS:** Release of emotions, intuition and communication.
- **SKIPPING WITH A ROPE – BENEFITS:** Grounding, creativity and confidence building.
- **WEIGHTLIFTING - BENEFITS:** Strength, empowerment and resilience.
- **YOGA – BENEFITS:** Balance, flexibility, holistic wellness.

Notes and Observations

10. ACTS OF KINDNESS; GIVE WAY – LET THEM THROUGH

However small, an act of kindness always goes a long way. If you are prepared to go the extra mile and not expect anything in return, you are existing on a high vibrational frequency.
You have experienced times when it has been tough, but you'll always remember the circumstances of when you were supported and helped out of a sticky situation. Giving back doesn't have to be done to receive.
Give way, flash your lights when someone gives way to you and exchange energy on a kind, respectable and peaceful vibration - always.
Occasionally as you give way, the other person may not respond or thank you. In these circumstances you could go down the negative vibrational route by showing your annoyance and letting them know you aren't happy that they didn't respond. This may lead to resentment, disappointment in their response, thinking it's a personal dig at you etc. Remaining calm and just letting this go is the high vibrational response. You may have found someone who was experiencing a bad day. Remember it's how you react to a situation, rather than the actual circumstance.

Sunday Drivers:
Why not take a leaf out of the book of the "Sunday Driver"? Instead of driving hell for leather at full pelt to get to your destination, try slowing down a bit and begin to focus on the views, and concentrate a little bit more on your pleasure rather than rushing and racing along. By going through life at such great speed, your Soul is missing out on so much.
As previously mentioned, this existence is an experience. It's much harder to immerse yourself in the experience if you don't take the time to appreciate and soak up all the highs and lows you will witness along your journey.
The "Sunday Driver" always appears to be taking their journey that bit slower, that bit more cautiously and with that a bit more of an appreciation of their surroundings.

Yes, they may be frustrating to drive behind, but they are probably returning home with a full immersion of a fantastic trip out that has given them the opportunity to be more mindful and less boy racer through life. Why not follow these "Sunday Drivers" and contemplate that the journey of life is precious and fragile. They know that by approaching that tight corner with caution or recognising the speed limits and appreciating the views – the journey is less of a rush and more of a peaceful, leisurely drive out.

11. CRYSTALS
– POSITIVE CHIPPINGS ON THE ROAD

Crystals are Earth's sparkly gifts that just keep on giving. Not only have they been created by minerals and natural phenomena, but they are also formed in an order that is highly structured. What appears to be random has been purposefully constructed. Each of its components carry various healing benefits for your human vehicle.

All crystals are vibrating on their own personal vibrational frequency. This frequency is high and the process of aligning with a crystal is rather like finding a car that matches all the positive reviews in a car magazine.

Some positive words that best describe a car or a crystal could be - Classic, limitless, luxury, beyond compare, advanced, sleek, curvaceous, ultra, powerful, tuned, enhanced, dynamic and futuristic.

When entering a crystal shop, it is much the same as entering a car showroom. The elite and shiny new vehicles of energy are all presented to you under complementary lighting. Your vibrational frequency will match with a harmonious crystal that will align with your frequency at that current moment. There'll be one that shines that little bit brighter, that calls you over to look at, to touch and to hold. The simple purposes of crystals are dictated by your frequency at that time and the properties they contain, so you can work together in a beneficial, healing partnership.

Crystals to enhance the driving of your car……

- Black Tourmaline – This is ideal for idling along as it not only protects you, but others. It can also assist with any bouts of road rage!
- Selenite – This crystal cleanses your energy and helps to relieve stress, encourages calmness and mental clarity.
- Clear Quartz - This will surround you with white light and clear your mind from any foggy, negative energy.
- Amethyst – This will assist in promotion of safe travels by promoting good health on all fronts; physically, mentally and spiritually.
- Smoky Quartz – This helps to keep you grounded and reduces overwhelm.
- Tigers Eye – This will assist with concentration, keeping you alert and focused and promotes ease in any decision making.
- Malachite – This will help protect you from any dangers from other's energy fields you may come into contact with. It is highly energised and will keep you going for long lengths of time.
- Carnelian - This advocates confidence and focus. It will protect you from accidents and near misses.
- Rose Quartz – This helps you to feel calm, balanced and less anxious.

Once you have returned from purchasing a crystal, (or two!) and to maintain the consistency of the crystal's power, it's worth following the advisory below in maintaining the cleansing and charging of your positive buddies and to bear in mind where you keep them as well. It's essential to be mindful of what levels of vibrational frequency you expose them to as they absorb the positive and not so positive energies; just like you.
By cleansing and charging up your crystals, they will maintain their potent, natural vibrancy for that bit longer.

Cleansing your crystals:

- Smoke Cleansing: Using a smouldering herb such as white sage, or Palo Santo, allow the smoke to cascade and swirl around the crystal(s). Visualise all negative energy leaving the crystal in the smoke.
- Water Cleansing: Hold your crystal under running water such as a stream or waterfall for a few minutes while setting the intention that any negative energy is washed away. Be aware that some crystals are water soluble and can dissolve, such as: Gypsum, Fluorite and Malachite.

Charging your crystals:

- Sunlight Charging: A very powerful method of charging your crystal is to place your crystals in direct sunlight for a few hours to allow them to absorb the strong, energy of the sun's rays. There are certain crystals, however, that may fade in direct sunlight for too long such as Amethyst and Rose Quartz.
- Moonlight Charging: Place your crystals in a space with full exposure to the moonlight. The full moon is especially potent for this. It will enrich your crystals with calming, cleansing energy.

Warning(!) Once you start collecting crystals, there isn't a handbrake strong enough to hold you back from regularly investing in them!

Notes and Observations

12. "CAR BUMPER STICKER" – BE KIND TO YOURSELF

Be kind
to yourself

You tootle along in your daily routine considering the feelings of others and it could well be that you sometimes forget about yourself. Always treat yourself with the utmost love and care that you deserve.

If you struggle with this, when negatively chastising yourself inwardly, imagine that you are talking to a small child instead, and then consider the way in which you would interact with that small human. How would you chat, encourage and praise that youngster if they were chastising themselves?

It's a bit like kicking the tyres and the bumper falling off! If you don't treat yourself with kindness and love, over time, function will diminish, and bits of you will begin to well and truly weaken!

Don't let yourself be the "obstruction" on your road ahead. In the long run this is not going to benefit your spiritual growth, and you may create a blind spot for moments that you have missed by listening to your negative chatter and acting upon it or prioritising people pleasing above your own well-being. You'll know this has occurred when it feels like everyone around you appears to be moving on and grasping opportunities that you may have decided, (wrongly) you didn't think you could or should do. Low self-esteem over time can begin to become your internal narrative. All the negative jibber - jabber and the "what if?" scenarios that your mind can conjure up for you before you have even given something a try. What is the cause of your reluctance to get out there and live your life to the fullest?

Is it fear of failure?

Is it fear of being ridiculed?

Fear is a very strong emotion. Remember though, that it is energy in motion. Fear can make you feel worried, anxious, doubtful, panicked and terrified.

Work with the fear and let it flow through you energetically. By doing this you are recognising any physical symptoms and understanding why you are responding in this way. A little fear or nervous energy will shift and propel you and create a flow if you allow it to. Resentment of those who have been that bit braver than you will drain your energy. The emotion jealousy is a good example here. It is your Soul at a crossroads. Do you take the road of resentment and sit in pain, feeling powerless and allow opportunity to pass you by – not the high vibe you're aiming for remember - or do you accept this as a guide. An opportunity to use the fear to your advantage. It's malleable and you can get some fantastic results if you acknowledge, but don't hide from it. Emotions are your little pointers on the road map of life. Indicating when you are unbalanced, unaligned, balanced or aligned. You may have suppressed them in order to not upset the apple cart or you may have used them to power you on through tough times. Getting to know your emotions and when they fire up will help you in regaining some self- esteem and maintaining a good balance when expressing them.

Advisory

ADVISORY: How to "drive through" those massive emotions:

- **Stop the engine and apply the handbrake - just pause. Acknowledge the emotion's presence and give it some space and time.**
- **Recognise the emotion in and around your body. Where do you feel it? Is it in your stomach like a cramp? Is it a tightening in your jaw? Is your heart thumping in your chest?**
- **Put a name to the emotion – e.g. "I feel sad/anger fear/envy.**
- **Know that you are safe, and that this emotion will pass.**
- **Consider its cause. What occurred that made this emotion pay you a visit? Recall what happened right before it appeared?**
- **Untangle its message – why is it visiting? What is the message it is trying to give you? What needs does it feel are not being met?**
- **Start up the engine again and act. Decide how you will react and respond to the emotion.**
- **Let it go when you feel you are ready, allowing it to leave you in a safe way that is personal to you. Then continue on your journey, accelerating gently away.**

13. RUNNING IT INTO THE GROUND - (IN A GOOD WAY!)

Parking up in your comfort zone, could be a tempting option. Its familiar, comforting and safe. Often if feeling a little unbalanced or overwhelmed, your comfort zone does exactly that. Zones you out and comforts you from too much stimulation, confrontation or vulnerable moments.

The advisories throughout this guidebook often suggest taking time out, reducing stimulation, recharging your energy etc. However, as it is all about maintaining the balance, too much of a good thing can sometimes have an adverse effect on your equilibrium too. You can start to feel sluggish, exhausted and even somewhat anxious to face the many adventures that are beyond the boundaries and restrictions of the comfort zone. Lack of stimulation can take you down a whole new journey and often the busy traffic of your mind chatter, will start to take over and may cause depression, unease and mind congestion.

Instead, consider the comfort zone more of a time restricted parking space. You know the ones. Usually at supermarkets or shopping complexes. Your registration is recorded and as long as you don't exceed your time limit and use the premises; all is well, and you won't get a huge fine for overstaying! Stay long enough, but don't depend too much on the fact there isn't a visible traffic warden - you are still being internally observed!

So, after the recharge and time in the session restricted parking space, unfurl your wing mirrors, get yourself out there and take some risks. Embrace every moment, opportunity, experience and chance that you encounter, with full throttle and high horsepower. Nourish and fuel your Soul with excitement, joy and a smidgin of fear.

Remember how powerful fear is energetically, and if correctly used can get you out of many a near miss and scrape but also it can propel you to a situation that you perhaps didn't think you were brave enough to experience. You feel a tad out of your depth, but there's something in the background that is somehow encouraging you on. To pursue this activity would mean the outcome and experience would out do the fear and uncertainty.

Visualise a positive outcome rather than what could go wrong, think about all the things that could go right. How it would make you feel and the pride in overcoming the obstacles you may have put in your own way.

Run your vehicle into the ground by grasping every opportunity that comes your way. Say yes to the many moments of excitement and fun that is out there, if you seek it and don't shy away from. There'll be plenty of time to park your car up in the garage and leave it there when the time comes. For now, though, begin the process of embracing the life that you are currently experiencing in a safe (though not too safe), balanced and joyful way. Once you have the memories to look back on, these positive experiences will continuously fuel your Soul.

Movement moves your energy. Energy doesn't go anywhere; it just transmutes and changes to suit the frequency. If you don't move regularly, or occasionally leave your comfort zone, the flow of energy will become blocked and lifeless. This is when obstructions will occur and your energy level is overwhelmed, cluttered and fragmented, causing you to feel regretful, envious and generally tired of life.

Allow the endorphins to travel through you and pep up your Soul. Your Soul is calling out to be taken on a magical mystery tour, a road trip into unknown territory, a stimulating adventure. Something you've always wanted to do but not had the courage to try. Immerse in the freedom of movement and new experiences, to give your body and Soul a fantastic gift.

Purely in a metaphorical sense – take yourself on a joy ride, do some engine revving and handbrake turns with life.

Much of your childlike excitement about life has most probably been supressed but it hasn't left you really, it's just hidden within.

Joy is a very high vibrational frequency emotion remember, and when you have the opportunity to tap into it, try to maintain it for as long as possible.

Search for the child within and give yourself permission to not take life so seriously. Find that inner giggle and the bouncy, light, fun, charismatic vibration and with none of the hard edges.

Ensure you give yourself a jaunt away from the confines of your home, your job or your car.

14. "PAWS ON BOARD" PET THERAPY- EXCHANGING AND MAINTAINING POSITIVE VIBES

Be it paws or claws, an indoor pet or a wild bird – animals hold a unique energy, that serves you, aligns with you and can even calm and change your mood for the better energetically, while you are with them.

When you pause with your pooch or pat your purring puss, there is a conversation going on between you, that has no words. You begin to use your other senses when interpreting what that look means, what that meow meant. Are they happy or unwell? You unconsciously are stripping back every usual means of communication and instead, working with their energy, their behaviour, their stance, their body language, their Soul.

Not only are you communicating with them on an energetic, non-verbal level, but you are also ensuring they are giving back to you many rewards as well. The beautiful thing is that there are no strings attached in this relationship. The dog wishes to please you, the cat will sooth you on your knee, the budgie will offer song and company, the rabbit an entertaining, playful fluffy handful, the fish in the tank performing in its own little live action movie, the songbirds in the garden offering music and pleasure, or the pony that gently carries your load. As you give to your pet or wild bird you too shall receive.

Building a precious rapport with your pet is a relationship that can only be fully experienced by giving your whole self to them. The more you give, the more you will receive – and all on a high vibrational energy frequency too!

There is that sense of knowing between you, of trust. The various personality traits and the soft, gentle demeanour provides calming, soothing responses from you. It's known that having a pet can lower your blood pressure, offer you company when lonely, reduce your stress levels and enable you to focus and take a little time out from the busyness of everyday life.

Bird watching is another way of experiencing mindfulness. Watching the varieties of birds going about their everyday routines, and allowing you to focus on the colours, the feather formations and birdsong can bring so much pleasure too. You could take it up as a serious hobby and get out and about in nature as well.

The trust that you build will not be forgotten by your pet either. They'll be picking up and tuning in to your tone of voice, every raised volume, every movement you make and your eye contact. The confidence or fear you emit will be picked up by them – therefore treating all animals with the utmost respect is so very important and a very basic role the human being has to play. Your exchange of energy will be of a potent, high vibration and full of profound healing, as long as you maintain a healthy, loving relationship with your fur babies at all times.

MOT FINDINGS

So, it's now time for you to come and collect your keys and pick up your car from the MOT Station for your Soul. Take this opportunity to take a deep breath in and contemplate on your feelings at this very moment and breathe out any tension within.

Right now, how do you honestly feel? Has some of the information resonated, surprised you – shocked you even? Perhaps your perception has changed – shifted. You are now observing more from above rather than below. The lovely thing about growing and developing spiritually, is that it isn't a race. You will go at your own pace and discover little forks in the road and turn offs that are unique to you. It could be that the little prompts have stirred something within, that you didn't know was there. In fact, it has always been there, it's just it was momentarily forgotten.

A lot of your life may have been conditioned into believing something that wasn't quite aligned with your thoughts and beliefs, but due to the conditioning, you followed the others and believed it to be true, as no one was questioning it, least of all you! Part of developing spiritually is to begin to question more and to really feel the energy peaks and troughs. To understand that every experience is a learning experience and is for your development; is a huge learning curve. That it's not happening <u>to</u> you but <u>for</u> you is probably the most important thing to remember from the MOT.

It could be that you now feel prepared enough to begin your journey of self-discovery and healing. Healing all the parts of you that you thought to be YOU but were actually residual pockets of energy that got a bit stuck, blocked and attached along the way. With the knowledge and tools offered here, you

can gradually start to shift some of the layers and maintain a soft, gentle high vibrational frequency on a constant trajectory.
This is a Mode of Transformation and as you spiritually develop, grow and transform, you can return again and again for the advisories travelling through this section.
Do you feel the same as when you lifted the bonnet of curiosity at page one?
As with every journey to a destination you will be going at your own pace and following the road of your choice. The road map of healing and then to an energetic frequency that you can comfortably maintain, is within your reach, but the road can be a challenging one. You may feel that you are not quite ready, this too is absolutely ok and understandable. You may wish to park up your vehicle and continue just as you did before.
Have there been elements that you'll pass on and overtake on the outside lane? They just didn't hit the mark and at this current moment in time, you don't feel they aligned with your thoughts or your needs.
Yet, if you were to look back on your experiences during the MOT, and there was something that your Soul flashed its headlights at and really resonated with you, would you consider travelling on that bit further?
A spiritual journey is unique and personal to you and your Soul. There are no hard or fast rules, highway codes or road restrictions in how you go about growing and developing spiritually.
Check in on your original Diagnostic Soul Survey results from when you first started this book. Would you say that they have improved or not changed at all?
Take on board the advisories, return to them when necessary and remember it is an energetically transmuting process rather than an accelerated dash.
Whatever the outcome, hopefully this particular MOT experience, didn't cost you too much, and all the advisories, will be of benefit to you and Your Soul, in the long run!

SECTION 2 – Service for your Soul

Not only is this section your handy road map for navigating some of the many ups, downs and tight corners that you may encounter on life's journey, but it also lays down the asphalt, concrete and tarmac on the road ahead of your spiritual awakening.

Start your engine and allow "Service for Your Soul" to drive you in the direction that won't have you veering towards dead ends, cul-de-sacs or no-through roads, but one that guides you towards open, never ending high - ways. A route that you may never have considered to head down until now.

Like the service for your car, you'll find there are more in-depth checks on the overall health and wellbeing of your human vehicle. Advisories and suggestions that steer you from any negative influences, low energetic frequencies and old thought patterns. Instead, encouraging and advising you on the many modes of how you can travel through life on a high vibrational freeway, and at your own speed. Offering you an alternative route that your Soul has been gently manoeuvring you in the direction of for some time. One that leads you towards empowerment and enlightenment.

Mind, Soul and Body Check

Your Precious Automotive

LAYOUT OF CAR AND CONTROLS

Your Soul is untethered, yet at this moment in time; securely seatbelt clasped into your vehicle, for this particular jaunt out. Your Soul is your essence, your true being, the authentic you. The untarnished, unprogrammed, impartial, tolerant, high praise, high vibe, illuminating, brilliant, energetic life force that is YOU. Your Soul radiates love, light and joy. Your Soul is unique, inquisitive and confident. It's the force of energy that is connected to all other living Souls. Who you meet, who you associate with, who you choose to form any relationship with; it guides and drives you along the twists and turns of life. Your Soul is your higher self, your chassis, encapsulated within a protective framework of the panels that are your human flesh and bones
Your Soul's power is eternal and will continue on, in many shapes, and guises; long after you've left this one at the scrap merchants. It might even be that you trade your Soul in for a new saloon, - but that's a whole new thought process, maybe for another time!
Your Soul is part of a network within, that continues to exist and power on. It has adapted and transmuted into the confines of a human body, this time! Entering with the impression of the mileometer set at zero, but in reality, has clocked up a fair few miles, and is searching for more opportunities to grow and evolve. Your mind has simply accepted it as seen.

I'll let you pull over and park up with that just for a moment....

As you read on and begin this very personal expedition, it may seem like you have just entered a tunnel of mystery and self-discovery. One that you didn't know you were heading towards, and you feel a sense of uncertainty about how long you might be driving through it, yet instinctively you know that there isn't any means of turning around, you just have to keep on going.

The rules of this road are to give yourself permission to enter the slip road of realisation and then join the carriageway of remembrance. It can be a very lonely road, and one of steep inclines and low-grade slopes. Many a moment of testing your brakes and seeking the nearest lay by to comprehend your trip. Take this moment to contemplate that not only are you a human being you are also an energetic being and your existence requires maintenance. To fulfil this, your Soul needs you to be consistently "tuned into" a source of high-vibrational frequency.

Your Soul has entered the vehicle of your body and as with any new car, the overall new and exciting aspects of a fresh mode of transport will eventually wear off and as you get used to the biting point, the clutch, the sharpness of the brakes, and the shiny new wheel trims, everything will start to feel comfortable and easier. However, to reach that point, your Soul will have experienced a great number of situations, circumstances and test runs around the block and have been fully immersed in the familiarity of what it is like to reside in a human being.

Upbringing, one's self-esteem and social acceptance plays a big part in how you maintain a consistent high energy frequency and keep your fuel level high.

You may have been encouraged to think towards your future, those life goals, work deadlines or holiday plans for example. Or prompted to look back at the past, the mistakes, regrets, and embarrassing, awkwardly memorable moments. Perhaps you haven't been inspired to live in the here and now with quite the same veracity.

Of course, the future hasn't happened yet. To an extent, you can plan to ensure something organised occurs as problem free as possible, but part of living a high vibrational existence is the acceptance that you don't have any control over the route you take to where you are heading.

You still have an arrival point, but environmental issues, unforeseen circumstances, or illness may put pay to the future turning out exactly how you hoped it would. Rest assured though, if you were meant to be where you finally end up, no matter what route was taken, then that was the way it was always meant to happen. If the energy flows with ease and is trouble free, then you are certainly on the right road.

Three of the main causes of lowering the energetic frequency are stress, anxiety and overwhelm. It's beneficial to understand why your physical body reacts and responds in the way it does, and the effects it has on your Soul. Fortunately, these challenging feelings can be reduced and eased from your day-to-day experiences.

If you tend to drive over the bridge before you've even arrived, this will deplete your energy. You are overworking your mind, and all the used-up energy means that the stress can take over and start to overwhelm you. Just like revving your engine can cause damage, it's advisable not to exceed the safe limits. This may lead to a panic attack which is an emotional response based on fear.

Advisory

To prevent overusing your energy, try to bring yourself back to the now. Focus on five things you can see, hear, taste, smell and touch. Your mind prefers an alternative activity to concentrate on and this will cause those anxious thoughts to be temporarily forgotten.

Knowledge and acceptance of anxiety as natural, and "human" has a calming effect on your inner engine. It takes away the pressure of believing it must be you, your character or personality that causes anxious reaction. Just knowing you are not the cause of the situation, that your reaction is completely natural, allows you to go about your life with less fear and more acceptance. The tools in this section show you, that all you experience will benefit your Soul and encourage spiritual growth.

The more you learn how to navigate through anxious experiences, you will both reduce their frequency and the level of anxiety. Getting this right, allows your Soul to experience more highs. The lows brought on from unnecessary physical symptoms of totally non-life- threatening situations, will no longer trouble you.

Let's go a bit deeper here, and look at the physical shell of your vehicle:

The way your physical body has been wired up is pretty basic and it hasn't had an upgrade since Souls were beginning to start their first ever human road trip. Back then, the human's main concern was about the survival of their species. Instinctively, survival mode would kick-in.

A bit like Sport Mode, this would prepare the vehicle for acceleration to avoid being a bear's or sabretooth tiger's next meal! This process creates a stress response.

There are 3 physiological responses.

- Flight: Putting your pedal to the metal and getting yourself away from the threat as quickly as possible.
- Fight: Fighting off the threat.
- Freezing: When you are so overwhelmed with stress you are literally immobilised.

On a physiological level, your body is preparing to respond to a situation in the way it deems appropriate. In either the flight or fight responses, you discard any waste, to allow for full potential to removal yourself from harm or fight it off. Hence, when nervous there are plenty of bathroom trips before the concerning event!

Your heart rate will accelerate due to the increase in the hormone adrenaline (this is comparable to over revving your car), and you'll experience a surge of energy, making your breathing race and your limbs feel restless. In freeze mode you are on super alert, yet in a state of immobilisation. When this mode kicks in, the physical body is saving energy as movement would be too dangerous.

Briefly we are going to look at the Electronic Control Unit now:

On a psychological level you have logged all the emotions associated with feeling unsafe, and in a split-second decision, have physiologically responded in a way that suits a life-threatening experience, even when really there isn't one. The experiences of the past have embedded into your subconscious. Your subconscious keeps you physically safe and works with the nervous system. It reminds you when you felt threatened, in danger or there was a potential that you were going to be harmed and has messaged your brain to get into which ever mode of response would work best.

Unless you are in a genuine situation that would endanger your survival (your body won't let you down with this as it's a vintage, and honed method), you are left with the residual energy that would have been used to run from or fight off a predator. Each time this response is triggered in situations where actual flight or fight is not required, you add more to the tank of residual energy. This built-up energy is difficult to fully release.

An inability to release pent up physical and emotional energy can manifest into varieties of overwhelm, anxiety, panic and feeling out of control. As none of these are pleasant experiences, the fear of any returning, causes the subconscious to go into overdrive once more and the cycle begins again.

Your subconscious still wants to protect you and has adapted to a new predator dressed in the form of the dentist or an important exam for example! The physical response of your body hasn't changed and will react just as it did for your past ancestors, when the threat to life was more commonplace. The modern world has continued to keep moving and changing, yet the very basic wiring of you has yet to catch up.

Hot Wheels

Vibrational frequency refers to: "the speed at which an object or system vibrates around a central point. The faster the speed, and faster the vibration, the higher the energy." Human vibrational frequency refers to your overall state of wellbeing, energy and consciousness. Metaphorically, how well your engine is running.

Your human vehicle contains energy points within your body that when fully functioning, are like wheels spinning on their own axis, they can spin fast or slow. Known as Chakras (Chakra is a Sanskrit word meaning Wheel), they will spin in relation to the energy level of the system and are part of a large network of subtle energies. Chakras work alongside and correspond with elements of your inner engine and ensuring they spin freely, will mean less effect on your emotional and physical wellbeing.

Chakras work with multiple sets of issues on a physical, emotional, and spiritual level. They are the components of the human energy system. Imagine them as your car's hard drive. Each energy wheel remembers every physical, emotional, and spiritual experience, and each has a particular role to play.

Living cells from you, animals and plants emanate an unseen energy. Unique cells that incarnate your physical organs, generate ordered energy patterns. Your body's system works in harmony with your breathing, circulation, digestion, reproduction, and secretion elements. There are 6 conforming Chakras for those physical events.

Your brain and your whole being has one Chakra, giving you a total of 7 major energy wheels within.

They are situated above your head, forehead, throat, heart, solar plexus, the navel and at the bottom of your pelvis.

The seven major Chakras are:

1. ROOT– Located in the tail bone area. Colour: Red. Works with the large intestine and the rectum and is related to the adrenal gland. Its meaning is physical identity, stability, family, fears of abandonment, personal security, support, loyalty, and grounding. **The Root Chakra is aiming to free and release negative energy. It promotes a sense of grounding, security, and stability. It's often used for overcoming fear, guilt and other emotions that may obstruct personal growth.**
2. SACRAL – Located just below the navel. Colour: Orange. Works with the reproduction system, reproductive organs, bladder, and kidneys. Its meaning is sexuality, pleasure, creativity, fear of losing control, blame, guilt, casual and intimate relationships, **The Sacral Chakra is believed to echo with emotions, creativity, and passion. It helps with breaking negative patterns and implementing positive changes. Its frequency is associated with freedom from any past traumas and promotes a harmonious flow of energy.**
3. SOLAR PLEXUS -- Located in the stomach area. Colour: Yellow. Works with the liver, gall bladder, stomach, spleen, and small intestine. It's related to the pancreas. Its meaning is self-esteem, confidence, trust, fear, ability to manage crisis, strength of character, worries over physical appearance, and your personal honour code. **The Solar Plexus Chakra is to promote healing and transformation, harbouring love, and compassion. Its frequency of healing is associated with DNA repair and is used to promote balance and positive energy.**

4. HEART – Located in the centre of the chest, just above the heart. Colour: Green. Works with the heart and the arms and in relation to the thymus. Its meaning is love, compassion, hope commitment, fear of loneliness, grief, and anger. **The Heart Chakra, aims to enhance communication, understanding and harmony in relationships. This chakra is used to promote compassion, forgiveness, and the healing of emotional wounds.**

5. THROAT - Located in the throat. Colour: Blue. Works with the lungs and throat and corresponds with the thyroid gland. Its meaning is communication, choice and strength of will, faith, knowledge, following your dream, personal expression. **The Throat Chakra focuses on self-expression, clarity, and communication. Its frequency is often used to promote problem solving, enhance intuition and stimulate personal growth.**

6. THIRD EYE - Located between the eyes, on the forehead. Colour: Indigo. Works with the pituitary gland and is related to the brain, face, eyes, and nose etc. Its meaning is intuition, self-evaluation, truth, intellectual abilities, emotional intelligence, and imagination. **The Third Eye Chakra is associated with intuition and spiritual insight. Aiming to activate and open the Third Eye, enhancing perception and intuition. Often used in meditation practices to deepen spiritual awareness.**

7. CROWN - Located above your head. Colour: Violet does not have a corresponding organ but is connected to the whole being – your courtesy light. It is connected to the pineal gland. Its meaning is awareness, your connection to your spiritual nature, ability to trust life, selflessness, faith, inspiration, devotion, and spirituality. **The Crown Chakra is associated with oneness, cosmic consciousness, and spiritual connection. Its frequency is often used in spiritual practices to elevate consciousness and promote a sense of unity with the universe.**

Notes and Observations

Gear Shifts

Engagement and disengagement with the connection of your Soul.
You leave the "showroom" all shining and unmarked. Not yet driven. Not yet taken on any road trip. The interior is fresh and unblemished. All is new and original, unique and unfamiliar.
Just like a car, as you leave the safety of the forecourt, (your mother's womb) you are now here to begin your journey.
As you grow and develop, you are exposed to many influences. Both positive and negative. Countless rules and regulations ensuring your health and wellbeing is safe and maintained to a sufficient degree, in order for you to continue existing. During your early, developmental years, you were like a sponge at the bottom of a valet's bucket, soaking up every piece of information, every good, bad and not so pleasant element of growing and developing into an adult.
By the time society has confirmed that you are an adult, you have experienced numerous encounters with countless, varied, energies. Like an air filter, there is only so much that you can catch, purify and strain away, before it starts to have an effect on your overall wellbeing.
You will have met people whose energy matched your vibration, ones who only wanted what was best for you, with no tow ropes attached. You will have met those whose energy made you feel uncomfortable and unsafe, those that made you feel heavy and unable to express yourself comfortably.
You will have encountered energy where you truly wanted to be with that Soul forever and always and energies that you want nothing more to do with. These are all encounters for your Soul to learn and expand from and will continue throughout the rest of your existence here on earth.
Your time here, is for you to gain the relevant experiences, to learn from

the knowledge gained, create, mentor others and give your Soul as many opportunities as possible to grow.
Think of your time here as one long car theory test. Where you will be faced with similar situations, on a loop that your mind comprehends and accepts as being a "good day" or a "bad day". Or you "quite liked" them, but you "didn't really like" him. The spiritual lessons you are here to experience will remain a constant however, until the element of that particular test has been learnt and ticked off.
The many encounters you face will be travelling in a variety of different transport, but they will all have the same, subtle energetic vibration, for your Soul to learn from, or to mentor. You will learn that others operate their vehicles within their own beliefs and that from each experience, it's the way that you react, respond and deal with that experience that will achieve a "pass". When you have learnt what response is needed for that particular experience, then this will enable the process of spiritual growth. While on this educational journey you will encounter various energies that bring forward the lesson your Soul is here to embrace and develop from. Remember all Souls are connected so we are all learning together at different stages of our Soul's development.
To add a little oil into the mix - the most profoundly beneficial teachers you encounter may be wrapped in the body work of a parent, a friend, the boss or a partner, or even your own child. All these encounters have been scheduled in advance, and each energy plays its part in your learning experience. Even the postman has a role within your Soul "family". This is your chosen world, your chosen reality of existence. For the overall benefit of your Soul and for that of those you meet along the way.
You may unknowingly begin to start to become disconnected from your Soul, while trying to navigate your way through the twists and turns that you have come up against. Building a protective barrier when you feel let down or hurt, rather than investigating a little deeper as to why it makes you feel this way, and what can be done to improve the overall experience.
Without being aware, you have been powerfully manoeuvred and coerced into a particular way of functioning and exposed to challenging and demanding situations. As time goes on, you may gradually begin to lose some of the purpose, and awareness you left the showroom with.
You may feel that you have unwittingly been compartmentalised into certain social groups, an old and dense belief system or governed by those that appear to be more powerful than you. All of this can create a sense of separation from your Soul. Your engine is running but you're driving an automatic vehicle rather than a manual one. You're existing but for what purpose?
You may have been made to feel that to have a sense of empowerment and

autocracy is self- centred and selfish. As your Soul begins to flash its headlights for attention, you may begin to question the actions of the other road users around you, but the alternative route is unfamiliar and it's probably wise to stick with the familiar road – although this can often be challenging and miserable, it must be right. Right?!

Your natural, positive, courtesy light of vibrational energy gets draped with heavy layers of other people's thoughts, opinions and issues that start to become yours. Becoming more and more disconnected and losing yourself. You may feel that this suppressed, low energetic frequency must be the correct and conventional way to be.

How often have you been encouraged to believe that; "Luck is great, but life isn't meant to be easy, you have to earn your place here, luck has nothing to do with it," or "Life is always going to be hard work." Or "If you would only accept that life is hard, then things would be so much easier for you!"

Like paint used on the exterior of the vehicle to cover the scratches and dents, all of the knocks, hurtful, difficult, and emotional, negative situations and circumstances you have experienced begin to build a protective layer of debris upon your "courtesy light". The light that will always remain lit, but as described in section one, may flicker, dull or quietly fade.

When this happens, you become even more disconnected from your Soul, your true purpose and your energetic connection here on earth. Your energy field dims, and you continue on your journey, yet on such a low frequency of vibrational energy that you succumb to the belief that you are just a human. Your empathy and understanding for other Souls deplete greatly, and rather than feeling connected you feel that you are unbalanced and separate from others.

When disconnected from the Soul, you exist, just not to the fullest of your potential. In a sleep like existence. You may find that you follow the general flow of traffic, fear other people's opinions of you, feel scared to express an opinion, and are not confident in asking questions, preferring to be led instead and you are lacking in a voice. The silencer has well and truly been fitted to your exhaust!

Fear and shame are instilled into your existence, intertwined in your daily comings and goings and all that fresh, newness from the showroom has been replaced by a dull, tarnished, low energy frequency. Any negative thoughts are just as powerful as if they were spoken and can create your world the more you follow the route that encourages this dense, old and negative energy.

These situations will either quieten your engine or rev it up to discover the alternative routes you could take instead.

There will be some high-powered polishing required to buff up the dimmed courtesy light within and begin the process of healing. Eventually though, this will lead to you reconnecting with your Soul, existing on a higher vibrational frequency and fulfilling your true purpose, leading a multi-dimensional life, and fully understanding the reason you came to experience existence here on earth in the first place. In addition, you will reconnect with your Soul, and with the collective of all other Souls too.

When existing on a high vibrational frequency, not only are you ensuring that the energy remains lifted and light, but it also means that you are emanating love, and this is the intrinsic thread that is within us all and connects us all to an even higher source of energy. One that is constant and always dependable. As time goes on, and more of us reconnect to our Souls we will no longer be a lost, idling vehicle, unsure and stuck on a foggy road to nowhere, but will exist as a loving, confident, unique form of transportation that isn't restricted, follows their heart and has no fear of being able to be the true and authentic Soul that we came here to be. By taking on board the advisories in this guidebook you can start the process of reconnection. With intention, send your love rather than hate to all who need it energetically and endeavour to maintain a positive, reframed thought process that will let things go, and allow the positive energy to flow. This is a healing process. As you heal, those you are connected to you heal; and as we are all connected, we will all heal.

Overinflated Tyres

The Ego: a little bit above your "petrol station."

Wanting confirmation of your brilliance, fuels the ego but drains the high vibrational frequency.
People pleasing and not having strong, personal boundaries depletes the energy too. Balance occurs when the Soul and Ego exist in harmony and are aligned with each other.

The ego is the drive within that keeps on keeping on. A motivation station to start your engine every day. Sometimes though the balance can shift, and the ego can make you begin to look at your world in a tunnel visioned way. When the ego is overinflated, it convinces itself and you that it is more important and more brilliant than anyone else. By telling everyone how brilliant you are, you are fuelling the ego. It is reassured when someone else agrees and backs up the story. If your Soul is the courtesy light, then the ego is the nodding dog on the dashboard, getting over excited with every movement and sometimes falls off when taking a sharp bend. Always wanting the recognition for what has been achieved, when not getting sufficient reassurance, the ego is dulled and searches for new opportunities to be the centre of attention. The ego is quite hard to tone down, especially if it has travelled along automatically expecting recognition, accolades and acknowledgements.
Equally, if there wasn't some sort of motivation to keep your engine firing in a balanced way and the ego became so deflated that there wasn't a strong urge or push to drive you onwards – just like having a flat tyre – your vehicle will be in as difficult a position as with an overinflated ego.
To work in harmony, your Soul doesn't work exclusively with just the Self like the ego, instead – it looks at the bigger highway ahead. It considers all the

other vehicles it shares the roads with and contemplates how the journey can be as beneficial, trouble-free and joyous for you as it is for the next vehicle. Your Soul doesn't require the same level of reassurance as the ego, and they will work well together when aligned.

The ego has worked hard to be where it is right now. Though it can have a bit of an identity crisis at times! Its main function is to feel prestigious and renowned. The ego is trying to find gratification, security and love, that along your journey it may have missed out on. Your Soul can provide all three. By aligning the ego and your Soul, the ego is reassured enough and feels safe, secure and cherished and won't need to toot its horn for attention, quite so often!

The key differences between the ego and your Soul:

- Tone – Your Soul's tone is calm; the ego is loud and critical.
- Emotion – Your Soul brings peace; ego stirs up fear and doubt.
- Perspective – Your Soul focuses on possibilities; ego focuses on limitations.
- Timing – Your Soul feels timeless and immediate; ego often reflects past patterns and future concerns.

How to distinguish between the ego and your Soul:

- Pause and reflect - Take a moment to question your mind. Ask yourself, "Does this feel far-reaching or restricting?" Your Soul will feel like opening up, yet the ego will feel like it is tightening.

- Check in on your emotions - If fear, anger or insecurity are driving your thoughts, it's likely the ego. If you feel calm and grounded its likely to be your Soul.

- Test the feeling – Imagine acting on your decision. If it feels more peaceful, it's likely your Soul. If it feels heavy or full of doubt, it may be the ego.

- The ego fears vulnerability, your Soul does not. The ego is resistant to change, your Soul is not. The ego is defensive and blames, your Soul does not. The ego attaches itself to labels and stories, your Soul wants to let it go with the flow. The ego has a fear of failure, rejection and seeks out perfectionism, your Soul does not.

The Steering

RIGHTY TIGHTY LEFTY LOOSY

"It's okay to be wrong, but it's important to be accountable when you are corrected. Humanity matters."

Advisory

You don't always have to be right. You don't always have to prove that you are right. You are right in your truth, and the truth will come out, when it is the right time to do so. Equally, it's okay to be wrong and accept, move on and be accountable when you are corrected.

Humility is when you accept that on occasions, you may not always be 100% perfectly correct in your assumptions, decisions or opinions; if you can accept this with courtesy and not feel the urge to bombard any other Souls with your perfectly correct presumption, you are vibing high. When the time is right and aligned you will find that the answers will come, and you don't need to prove your point constantly, or expect a satisfying sense of gratification from saying; "I told you so!" **It really doesn't matter.**

This is the part of you that wanted to be buffed and polished on that occasion – the ego.

Of course, there will be times when you get uptight and frustrated when you don't feel heard, appreciated, or you may feel taken for granted, misunderstood or put upon. You may feel an overwhelming desire to prove others wrong and reinforce the fact that you believe yourself to be right! This is a common defence mechanism, where quite possibly there has been many a situation where you were accused of something you didn't do or say and you felt you weren't listened to, you now feel you have to defend yourself to get your point across, no matter what the situation. Like a scratch that needs touching up on the bodywork, you won't be satisfied until the tarnish is removed. However, for a moment park up those misconceptions before being tempted into blowing a gasket in frustration and the ego's need to be correct.

Within, your Soul accepts when a wrong turning has been made and ideally wants to let the energy flow freely with no blockages like self- deprecation, or harsh criticism, and knows that by giving space and time to the situation the truth will eventually come out, at the time it is supposed to. Rather than when the insecure ego is demanding it.

"A mystery will always be solved; truth will eventually and inevitably be discovered." (proverb)

Time and patience are required and that will take time and patience. Assertiveness however is your power. It is your right to protect your boundaries and your bodywork. No one has the right to dent, or puncture with their demands and unrealistic expectations of you. This is where strong boundaries need to be applied and maintained. They must always be consistent. Assertiveness is not anger or rage. Those are the emotions associated with having your boundaries crossed too often. Assertiveness is the protection of your precious energy. Like a car's air bag is to protect your head and face in a collision and the restraint from the seatbelt prevents collateral damage to your body; your energy air bag will activate and protect you from any draining demands, that will inevitably affect your body, mind and Soul. This can only be successful as long as the air bag is deployed at the right time and consistently. The intention is to protect your spiritual energy – your fuel from being drained. During the awakening process your energetic frequency is rising. Other Souls will either work with these changes or continue on their way. Remember that by keeping up a consistent, high vibration you are shedding dust and grime that has accumulated over the years. This is a gradual process and as you have been travelling along unknowingly with the layers of debris affixed, removing those first layers, will in the long run, support your Soul and give it permission to embrace the existence it came here to experience.

Potholes In Your Road

If you were never to encounter some potholes in the road, your Soul; that which is here to experience, learn, and evolve would not be able to expand in a useful, productive and all-encompassing way.
To fuel the Soul, it requires an assortment of different learning experiences, highs, lows and opportunities to open the doors to discovering your Soul's purpose while here on Earth. As you are starting to delve a bit deeper into this guidebook, you may experience some "Aha!" moments of confirmation. Moments that your Soul already knows, but you have only just caught up with the rest of you!

Advisory

The potholes or roadblocks you have experienced are not happening TO you but FOR you.

Through history there have been wars, disasters, carnage, accidents and awful atrocities. Each negative and bad reaction has a cause-and-effect on all Souls and has over time created dense and heavy energy. Yet by concentrating on your world, your personal battles that you have experienced and managed well, the positive vibrational energy from your experiences will reach out to others to gain knowledge and to learn from for their journey. This energetic connection will then travel out to the collective and assist in lightening the darkness for all Souls.
It may sound small, in the grand scheme of things, but you are such an important vehicle on this spaghetti junction called life, no matter how small your contribution is.
The response you present is going to affect the way you feel emotionally, and the way others feel too.

Your experiences, be they large or small, have had an outcome that you may believe should be shared - for the collective good of others. Your contribution will be useful for all Souls experiencing a similar situation, and the high vibration and energetic connection will be maintained.

For example, a car breaks down at a busy junction ahead and you have experienced something similar. You were aware of the frustration caused to the other drivers, however during your experience, a person came to check that you were okay, as opposed to them blasting their horn and speeding around you. You felt relieved and connected when someone stopped to assist so now by helping the stranded driver ahead, you'll be passing on a high vibe energy connection by going to see if they're okay.

Or a parent whose child was killed due to a speeding driver, campaigns for speed restrictions and through their grief, powers through until the restrictions are put in place and other children are that bit safer, therefore providing safety for future generations and some comfort that their child's death wasn't in vain.

All minor or major experiences can and do serve others and grow and develop your Soul, and everyone else's too.

As you allow this to gradually filter through, you'll notice less potholes and more freeway ahead.

It might seem easier to complain to anyone willing to listen about the "potholes" along your road, however, this is a classic example of lowering your energetic vibration and vibrating on a much lower frequency, when your intention should be to consistently vibrate at a higher frequency. Like a vortex the negativity will suck you down with it and your life experience will be lacking in drive and motivation – thus causing you to be stuck in a low gear. As you travel along this awakening journey, you'll be much more aware of negative talk. Try to hook into a positive element, no matter how small, to encourage the frequency to change. For your general psyche continuously engaging in a higher gear is the best option for most routes your Soul will take.

Reporting any potholes to the authorities and self-governing will mean action, advice taken on board, and absorbing techniques and coping strategies that are running through this book - means a less bumpy road ahead.

Seeking healing, will take you on a slight detour. You'll always get to the intended destination, but you are taking the long way round, or there's a heavy build-up of traffic on your route and it has meant the SAT NAV has given you alternative instructions. If you feel that your reactions to certain situations are detrimental for the free flow of your energy, then this alternative route will not just benefit you, but others too. Remember that your journey is unique to <u>your</u> Soul. It may be similar to others, but never exactly the same. Your connection to others means that your actions and reactions will have a ripple effect on those around you. Like throwing a hub cap into a pond, the effect of the action will cause a reaction.

Accepting that you cannot control everything that happens from day-to-day is one of the sharpest bends in the road, yet the most useful to know. Remember, it's the ego that is craving control as it feels unsure and insecure due to the unknown, and now this has put your subconscious into flight or fight mode. Your Soul already "knows" the route, but although the subconscious will learn to adapt in time, the ego is wanting to control elements that it is uncertain of. Both are wanting to protect your survival, yet one is more malleable than the other. This can often be a detriment to your Soul. Trusting in the process and your Soul is key here.

For example, you may have experienced situations that left you feeling vulnerable and triggered such unpleasant emotions that you now wish to avoid experiencing similar situations ever again. The way that the Soul needs to evolve however, is to feel that vulnerability again, respond in such a way that the outcome is a positive one and therefore reassure the ego. The subconscious is picking up on the emotions attached to the situation, and the ego is clinging on to the stories you have created surrounding the situation, not the actual experience. Therefore, you will never be able to avoid a situation, but you will be able to react differently, be more accepting, less triggered emotionally and gradually by doing this, the old emotions will be free to flow rather than remain attached. Just let it go. By freeing the blocked emotions associated with a situation the energy will move on and so will you.

It's a like rewiring the alternator, to create an alternative message. The more you do this, the more accepting your subconscious is and once happy with the diversion or alternative options, your ego will feel more secure, and this will create a less stressed existence. In doing so, you've begun to heal your little part of your world.

Take a deep breath and for a moment contemplate on all of the various challenges you've faced. The highs and lows, the ups and downs. The moments of paralysing grief. Remember how during all those experiences you may have felt that you were never going to get through it. That the hairpin bends were never ending. That the potholes and loose chippings that littered your highway would never clear. That your sense of calm and balance were so far-reaching that you didn't see a clear way through the unlit, foggy road ahead. Yet, as you sit here now, perhaps allowing yourself to remember certain situations, contemplate how far you have come, how much your Soul has grown and that you have managed to navigate those bends, travelled around the potholes and seen your way out of the depths of darkness. You've successfully managed your journey to reach this point, because right now, this

is exactly where you are supposed to be.
The tools intertwined within these pages, allow you to not be too hard on yourself, know that the decisions made led you to this point, but equally to be aware that there are alternative means of guiding you along a less hectic, energy zapping journey than you've been used to. A sort of fast track of knowledge. Wise words that allow you to arrive at this clear, calm and balanced destination in a quicker and more effective way. Anything that appears to stand in your way can be quickly and safely navigated and, as your Soul grows with experience and courage, what you may have thought were challenges can now be seen as gifts to you for your future self.

Road Ahead Closed
You know what it's like. You are heading home and there's an unexpected diversion sign, that will take you right around the houses before you can get to your destination.
You could look upon this as a nuisance, an inconvenience. The unplanned re-route that takes you on a journey out into the uncharted territory, a road less travelled. The unfamiliar places and unexpected twists and turns. It takes you out of your comfort zone and away from all things reassuring and safe.
Life will and often does create obstructions and an alternative route that perhaps you were not even contemplating, will unfold on your journey. This re-route may make you feel ill-equipped, and it may be challenging to enter the carriageway of the unknown.
There will, of course, be days when an unexpected situation or circumstance occurs. This is where your overall energetic strength needs to be at its highest level.
Energy transmutes to the frequency that dominates. The more you think negative thoughts, express negativity in voice or action, and "give up" on a situation, the more the energetic frequency will change to the one you are presenting.

The power is in your control. You have the unexpected diversion ahead, but the junction of choice awaits. Do you take the longer, different route? Embrace the fresh scenery, the extra time to contemplate and gather momentum, and get to your destination a little later but well and safe. Giving your Soul the opportunity to reassess situations, grow and develop or do you ignore the diversion and meet dead ends, road works, frustration and negativity?

Advisory

Allow yourself to absorb and process an unexpected situation. Various emotions will come to the fore and you must allow them to flow through you and out of you – the energy needs to keep moving.
As with any situation, they move away. Allow your Soul to take over and reassure you that in the long run, this is and will be beneficial.

Sometimes you need to immerse yourself in the vulnerability to receive strength and power. Overprotecting your vulnerability invites fear and worries the ego.
Your power needs to be regularly topped up to prevent falling so low that you can't see a way forward in your journey.
If you are regularly in the company of someone who is more negative energetically, then you will need to adapt accordingly as you will be more sensitive to their energy.

Advisory

You have no control over the hazards, twists and turns and snarl ups along your journey. You do have control in how you choose to deal with the hazards, twists and turns and snarl ups!
You are an amazing, creative being – so get creating! Create the road that you want to take. Just for you. This is your journey and creating a road that suits everyone else, and following the stream of traffic is going to obstruct that creativity.
There will be moments where you'll want to perform a U-turn, but rest assured, that you are not alone and are being guided and always supported.

There's a well-known American tv programme from the 1980's that involved all sorts of risks the two cousins took to avoid arrest from the County Sherrif! They'd even access their car in an extremely unconventional, yet creative way too! They'd speed along with no worries and mid-flight as they jumped over obstacles and other vehicles, rebel yell: "Yee-haw!!" Under the watchful eye of their uncle, the boys avoided any sanctions and lived their lives to the fullest! This is the high vibration you are aiming for! The wise Uncle is keeping his nephews out of too much trouble and is secretly pleased that his boys are biting the whole cherry off the top of life.

Okay, so maybe you won't put yourself in similar situations as them but use this as a metaphor. Have plenty of Yee-haw moments and engage your gears in creative, forward, driven thinking instead of driving along a worn away road, over-used by heavy vehicles and streams of cars following the same route.

Objects In the Rearview Mirror

Self-Reflection:
"Serious thought about one's character and actions". (Oxford English dictionary.)

The way you have been manufactured and assembled plays a critical part in how you are going to react and respond to a situation. Your main influences when growing up, have shaped you into what you are. You've accepted this naturally as being your normal, yet whilst self-reflecting on your whole being, a new journey will start to unfold; one that will reshape who you are. The ability to separate the residual energetic effects of your upbringing from that of your Soul's true essence is a critical crossroads to approach.
How you acknowledge and proceed with a situation is in your power. By self-reflecting you might recall many a situation that could have been handled differently by everyone involved. It could have been that you were snappy and impatient in the car on the journey home from work. You didn't get a thankyou from another driver who you had given way to. You then began chastising the other driver and as your anger built, it caused a red mist to overcome your decision making. Recall how this affected your concentration and how you treated other road users.
You might join a motorway and be cruising happily at a steady speed, then lights flash, the speed limit signs indicate 20 mph until further notice, and gradually the stream of traffic slows down to a standstill, due to an obstruction in the road. Do you weave in and out of each lane, hooting, flashing and preventing others in?
Perhaps you've returned home with a build-up of frustration and anger about how your day went. In this state you are unable to curtail your temper, and your loved ones are on the receiving end of your overheated engine.
Maybe, a planned trip has been cancelled due to unforeseen circumstances, and it means that you have to be more flexible in your actions, causing frustration. Think how this might cascade down into how you speak to others, due to your disappointment in the changed plans.

There will be many an experience both minor and major that you can refer back to – not all car related either - and accept that the way you responded in the moment had a far-reaching effect on where you are now and for those around you. Rather like leaving a car crash at the scene, if you don't attempt to take full responsibility for your words and actions when they have affected you and others, then you will be forever looking in your rear-view mirror on the look out to be pulled over.

Part of the human journey is to experience a myriad of emotions, as a human you experience life through your emotions (energy in motion) and by attaching a specific emotion to a negative circumstance, when a similar situation, phrase or behaviour occurs, you are triggered by the emotions that you attached to it at that time.

During the healing process, consistently practicing self-awareness and learning not to intentionally cause further hurt or harm to others or to yourself is paramount. By accepting that mistakes will be made along the way, your Soul has the opportunity to align with this positive frequency and this will allow the energy to flow faster and with ease.
Next time, do you ensure your fuel tank is sufficiently filled and make sure the road ahead is obstacle free by reflecting upon your actions, thoughts or words and where necessary, apologising for those situations? Or do you continue on an inflated ego but a deflated Soul?

The more you retune your frequency the more you will be aware of:

How you deal with situations, where in the past they may have escalated due to your reaction.

How another person's reaction reflects your own.

That you don't have to like everyone and accept that – guess what? - not everyone will like you.

Remember, it's nothing personal, it's different energetic frequencies. It's a meeting of vibration, nothing else. That which will attract or repel.

Underneath all of those many layers, we are all connected and ultimately striving for harmony while residing here on earth. On this particular highway, you are aiming for continual balance, thoughtfulness and consideration.

Think of when you're driving your car and how protected you feel from other road users. It may give you the edge, that bit more confidence to cut corners or even run other road users off the road who you believe are in your way. Yet the metal that is between you and the other road users can damage, scratch, crush and ultimately harm you if the car is driven erratically, without due care and attention or thought for other road users. You know the devastation left from a vehicle collision where in some circumstances the car is written off and unsalvageable.

As you've gone through all the many energetic experiences on physical, emotional and spiritual levels your vehicle's bodywork may need a little work doing to it and some panel beating to knock out any large dents – the really affecting stuff – out of your bodywork – Your energy field.

You may have reached a stage of breakdown, where functionality is difficult. Talking through the emotions to a therapist or energy healer will release the blocked emotions associated with past circumstances.

For more traumatic experiences your resulting overall condition, may require specialised, more long-term healing as the trauma experience may need time to be recognised and released in an environment where you feel safe, emotionally held and actively listened to, with no prejudgement.

This is where self-reflection plays its part. You are admitting to yourself that help is required to benefit you and others in the long term, but you have to make that decision yourself. No one else drives your vehicle. Until you decide that you need some form of healing to break through some of the negativity, to help you to understand yourself more and relieve you of any heavy burdens you carry, the healing process could take considerably longer.

Advisory

An emotion only lasts around 90 seconds. When the feeling arises, the body responds only briefly. Following that, it's not the emotion that lingers on, but the story you attach to it. By feeding the emotion with thoughts and replaying situations it seems like it lasts for much longer. The key is not to supress the emotion. Try not to feed the negative energy and notice when you are keeping the feelings alive.

EMISSIONS

You're having a bad day. You've created a garage in your head. The world seems against you. What comes out of your mouth wasn't meant to cause quite so much offence; yet the damage is done. As a human, your energy depletion can lead to impatience, snappy reactions and hurtful comments. These are the emissions that you are seeping out into the environment.

As you begin to gain more insight into why you may have reacted that way, the level of emissions you release will diminish too. Accept that this is part of experiencing being a human and no detriment to your character at all. That you are willing to work on yourself to reduce the toxicity coming from you, means you're beginning to get over some bothersome speed bumps along the way, with hardly any suspension issues.

Rather like being a witness to an accident, take on board all the elements of the situation that occurred from the stance of a third party. The more you act as the witness, the less likely you would want to emit toxins out into the atmosphere. You know how it makes the other person feel as you have felt it too.

Recognising that your intentions have caused hurt, and harm, is becoming more self- aware and an important part of the awakening journey and healing process. The knowledge that there are causes and reasons for why you reacted or responded the way you did indicates that you are conscious of how your inner engine works and why.

You will have been on the receiving end of an opinion, a negative comment or hurtful criticism. You may have taken this to heart and felt hurt and confused by your response. However, as you've discovered through this guidebook, emissions often get expressed when the energy is low or blocked, and there is nowhere else for it to be released. By maintaining a high frequency there is no reaction from you, and without reaction there will be no further action. It's the personal experience of whoever is emitting toxicity towards you. We are mirrors of each other and there may have been a trigger in your response that flooded their engine. Being conscious of this, means the negative energy and harmful emissions will disappear more quickly than taking on the energy of the person who is expressing their toxicity.

You are the catalytic converter in this situation. By not reacting you are releasing less harmful pollutants into the environment.

Back-firing: To swear or not to swear?
That is the question.

Interestingly, having a good swear may shift pent up energy and release any residual frustrated emotions. It may remove any blockages and will momentarily allow you to reset and move on. Yet language has only got a small part to play here. It is the energy frequency that you emit more than the words. Usually swearing is expressed at someone or something else, or even yourself. Occasionally it is an inanimate object that has got in your way. You know from personal experience that if you have been on the receiving end of someone's acidic rant, that you feel the heightened negative energy that creates hurt, anger, pain or other unpleasant emotions, these can cause frustration in you. That may make you cower in the corner or retaliate in equal measure with colourful language and insults.

In the context of a frustrating situation you may be in, the use of fruity language may be preferred. Crying out "Spanners!" rather than "sh*t" may seem an oddity, but unless you've had a bad experience with a spanner, the word is light, freeing and can be said in just the same way as a swear word, but the effect will be so very different on those around you and yourself. The energy will flow through you and allow you to release the pent-up energy, but not in a toxic manner.

Swearing is an outlet, that is all. You are frustrated, and like a car backfiring your fuel is combusting with a pop and a bang. Words have a vibrational frequency that either lift or lower the energy frequency. Swear words have been around a very long time and have evolved over time. They can be associated with negativity, toxicity and threat if used in a manner that is connected to anger and rage. If you've followed some of the advisories in the book so far however, you may not have such a strong urge to express your frustrations in this way.

Another low and old vibe practice is humour when used to harm others. When it is sarcastic, hurtful and insulting of someone else. This is when the ego is coming out to play once again.

Humour is an expression of joy, and used wisely, can put you and others at ease, release pent-up pressure and create a high frequency vibration, as laughter is the workout for mind, body and Soul.
Laugh rather than be consumed with embarrassment when you spill a drink over yourself or wave at the wrong person. In appropriate situations, break tension with humour and smiles rather than anger and snarls. It will lighten the energy and begin the process of your healing rather than wallowing in its negativity, which will take longer for the body to release. Clearly these are simple situations, but the effect of raising your energetic frequency via reframing your go-to thoughts, will have a positive effect on a situation.

Beware Of the Hitchhiker

When travelling along life's journey, you are going to encounter many a Soul who will flit in and out of your life. You'll exchange energy and go on your way. Generally speaking, that will suffice and simple interaction with most people will be an equal, healthy, to-ing and fro-ing of each other's energy. You and I and all living beings are energy and exist on various frequencies, so there will come a time when you experience an exchange of energy with a "Hitchhiker." An energy that hops in your vehicle uninvited and will begin to overwhelm the individual workings of your engine.

This could be subtle at first and you may not even have noticed that you have picked up an energy hitchhiker thumbing for a lift. You may be aware of feeling exhausted within yourself quite quickly, however when exposed to this energy for long periods of time. You may not get a look in as far as conversation and interaction is concerned. You may feel that you are regularly pleasing this person and not getting that much in return for your efforts. You may feel a bit used, deflated, or even tarnished after inadvertently allowing a hitchhiker into your mode of transportation. If energetically sensitive, you may also, without realising, allow this hitchhiker's thoughts, belief systems and personality traits to influence your vehicle, causing you to feel ungrounded, a little nauseous, overwhelmed and discombobulated.

These symptoms arise when your own energy is being pulled away from you towards the hitchhiker. There hasn't been the sufficient time to protect your own energy, or you were running on low fuel levels and they simply hopped on board, and any leftover energy is being drained, to refuel and top up their energy levels.

Now, to be fair, the large majority of energy hitchhikers are not conscious that they are draining you of your precious energy. Their energy frequency matches their current state that has been honed and developed over a long period of time. This is their ego tooting its horn, seeking reassurance and safety that for whatever reason, has been lacking. The energy hitchhiker will have no knowledge of how they might be affecting you energetically. As previously

discussed though, energy is subtle and as you continue on this journey of raising and maintaining your vibration, the energy of the hitchhiker is attracted to your positive frequency. Their ego is searching for security it is lacking from its host, and you are emanating it at this point, whether you are aware of that or not! After being in your company for a while, the energy hitchhiker will be feeling replenished, revived and good to go. They'll genuinely look forward to seeing you again very soon, as they always feel happy, content and well-nourished in your presence.
Your problem will be hidden and until you begin to understand that you are susceptible to allowing the energy that doesn't belong to you, into your vehicle; you won't be able to fully protect your precious energy, and your hitchhiker won't know any differently.

Hitchhikers come in many makes and models. You will still need to protect your energy, but the hitchhiker you only see on the odd occasion; waiting for a lift can be managed by ensuring your fuel gauge is high and your battery fully charged, then you can spare a little for this particular hitchhiker's encounter, as long as its only occasionally and you can replenish your energy using the tools mentioned throughout this book.

The main energy hitchhikers are:

1. **THE SUFFERER** – This type of energy hitchhiker is always running into problems and seeking sympathy. They often see themselves as constantly wronged by life and share their troubles repeatedly, always expecting support and reassurance. You may feel naturally that you want to help, but continuous exposure to their negativity will drain your fuel tank quickly.
2. **THE FAULT FINDER** – The fault finder is quick to point out imperfections and hardly ever has anything positive to say. Whether it's about your choices or general aspects of life, their constant criticism can chip away at your confidence and leave you feeling inadequate.
3. **THE SENSATIONALISER** – Sensationalisers love being the centre of attention. They often blow things out of proportion to ensure they remain the focus. Their exaggerated stories may seem entertaining at first, but over time, their need for drama can create an atmosphere of anxiety and agitation.

4. **THE DISAPPROVER** – Disapprovers have a habit of holding others responsible for their own troubles. They struggle to take responsibility for their actions and often find someone else to blame, this can create a frustrating and unfair environment, especially if you're often the one being aimed at.

5. **THE PUPPETEER** – The puppeteer is skilled in using emotional methods to get what they want. They might use guilt, pity or flattery, making it challenging to pick up on their true intentions. Interactions with puppeteers can be confusing and emotionally draining as you're often second guessing their intentions and your responses.

How to spot an energy hitchhiker: The 4 major signs.

1. **They need to be the centre of attention**: Energy hitchhikers often seek to be the main focus in social situations. They may frequently interrupt others, steer conversations back to themselves, or behave dramatically to ensure all eyes are on them. This constant need for attention is draining for those around them.

2. **They exaggerate problems**: Energy hitchhikers tend to blow things out of all proportion. A minor inconvenience might be described as a major disaster. A habit of exaggeration can create unnecessary drama and stress, making interactions overwhelming.

3. **They blame others constantly**: A key sign of an energy hitchhiker is their refusal to accept responsibility for their actions. They often blame others for their misfortunes and fail to acknowledge their own role in the situation. Being around someone who doesn't take accountability for how they behave can create a negative and unproductive environment, especially if you find yourself frequently being blamed.

4. **They use people**: These particular energy hitchhikers often view relationships in terms of what they can gain. They might manipulate situations to their advantage or take more from relationships than they give. Having a very unbalanced dynamic with a person can leave you feeling used and unappreciated, draining fuel from your tank.

How the energy hitchhiker might make you feel:

1. **Drained and tired** – One of the most noticeable symptoms of being around an energy hitchhiker is a sense of exhaustion. It's not just feeling physically tired – it's a deeper sense of being energetically depleted. You might find that after spending time with them, you feel you have very little energy left.
2. **Anxious or stressed** – Interactions with an energy hitchhiker can leave you feeling on edge. You might experience increased anxiety or stress, especially if you are anticipating future interactions. This can manifest into nervousness, irritability, or a constant feeling of tension.
3. **Avoiding social contact** – If you are regularly exposed to an energy hitchhiker, you might start to withdraw from social situations, even those unrelated to the energy hitchhiker. Isolating yourself is your mind's way of trying to retreat from the emotional drain.
4. **Overwhelmed by negativity** – Energy hitchhikers often have a negative outlook, and this can start to affect your mood. You might notice yourself feeling more pessimistic or less hopeful about things you used to feel positive about.

Advisory

Ten ways to protect your energy from hitchhikers.

1. Limit your exposure to reduce your fuel tank rapidly emptying.
2. Keep a mental distance to preserve your energy.
3. Establish clear boundaries on acceptable behaviours.
4. Avoid confrontations to minimise feeling drained.
5. Practice self-care by learning to say no.
6. Replenish your own energy through mindful activities.
7. Get a fresh perspective through a supportive chat.
8. Focus on the positives in your relationships.
9. Gain insights by educating yourself on relationship dynamics.
10. Seek support from a professional if it is impacting your life too much to manage yourself.

Advisory

Ensure to the best of your ability that you are fully recharged, and you are prepared to protect your energy and equilibrium by establishing some consistent boundaries.

Prior to leaving the home, to prepare for any encounters planned or otherwise with energy hitchhikers, imagine you are dressing in preparation for a car rally race. A race driver puts on protective gear, such as a helmet, gloves, suit and boots. To protect your energy field, put on your protective gear and envisage it as made from golden light. Your helmet flashes as it catches the sun, and the suit is intertwined with golden thread. While putting on your protective gear, say with intent this energy shielding affirmation:

"Please surround me with golden light today and shield my energy from all negative influence. Help me to keep my energy pure, clean and in high frequency."

Just like protecting the paintwork on your car you would apply wax, sealant and a paint protection film, as a human you would protect your body with clothes. This action is protecting your spiritual body from being exposed and vulnerable to harm.

Notes and Observations

The Classic Car Show

Maintaining a high energetic vibration on a constant route is immediately taken down a dead-end road when judgement and criticism of others enters your line of vision.

Whether you have a strong paint protection film or a chassis that can withstand different forces- it will have no bearing on how energy draining, the act of giving and receiving harsh criticism, picking faults about how someone else looks, their abilities, race, gender, sexuality and/ or character. This will take its toll and take you on a road that is now old, unkind on your suspension and unnecessary.

How do you scramble out of this situation? Ideally, the best thing would be to avoid the company of someone you know can be judgy, sarcastic and critical. If that isn't possible, be aware of what is being said and your reactions to it. If you feel strongly, challenge it. If you would rather not, then be mindful of not going down the road to nowhere with them. Don't respond or laugh as this is feeding their needs for any sort of response. As you become more aware of low energetic, vibrational frequencies you will feel it deep within. In your mind, send out to that person positive healing thoughts and understand that they are really criticising a part of themselves, that requires some mending. These are those who have been exposed to harsh criticism themselves, and it has, over time become the normal and accepted behaviour for them.

A judge at a classic car show is looking for a quality exterior and interior, mechanical quality, cleanliness, suspension quality and overall concept. They are guided by what they see and the quality of the vehicle. If the car doesn't meet the criteria, then it will lose points and probably won't win. While at the car show it's about looks, features and power. However, in this context you are not a car at a show, and you are not the judge of the best in show either. You are on your own unique journey. What is right for one, won't be right for you, the way you walk isn't the same as your neighbour or friend, the way you talk, the accent you have, the colour of your skin has no bearing on who you are as an energetic being. All your experiences are unique to you. You don't have to have anyone's permission to present to the world whichever way you so desire – just keep the vibe high.

When you have been brought up in or regularly exposed to an environment of harsh criticism and negative put downs, this could be the established norm, and take a while to push through the dark, low, heavy and old residual energy this way of being creates. Accept that there is no one higher or better than you, and there is no one lower or worse than you. We are all connected, on a Soul level. Like a mirror, every person you exchange energy with is reflecting all the good and not so good nuances and elements of you. Those that you are afraid to expose, yet as you see them reflected back at you can be challenging to accept and a harsh terrain to navigate. Hurting someone intentionally with your words and or judgement, is actually hurting you. You are saying these things because you have been hurt and are hurting.

The sad part is that you have been unwittingly towed down this road, believing it to be the right direction as no one has told you any different. The brilliant part is that you can bang on the dashboard of life and perform a U- turn. Create a you that chooses not to tolerate what most people think is the right route to take, and take a solo road trip, raising and maintaining a high vibe as you continue driving onwards from the old, stagnant, conditioned beliefs you may have picked up along the way.

Eyewitness - Idle Talk

"So.... What's the goss?!"

If you were to crash your car into a wall, there is only your interpretation of what happened. Unless there were witnesses who would have had their own account of what happened, or if you crashed into someone else; they too would have their own take on things - but if it was just you, your car, one wall - this would be your conscious perception of the incident, and no one else's.

If you were talking to someone else about the crash but you weren't involved in the accident or even at the crash scene, you are informing the other person of your perception of the accident. You have not got any facts as you didn't witness it happening, but you feel you have enough information based on your perception, that what you say is truth. Your truth. But in your mind the truth. So, the person you have told your version of the accident to, now has their own perception of it - although they weren't there either - and then that person will share their version - probably with some embellishments - to the next person, who will probably believe that person's account -but will accept it with their perception - and on it goes!

This is the formula for gossip. An energy draining activity that can have hardly any truth in it at all. Yet it does demonstrate how powerful energy can be, and how we are all connected both positively and negatively.

Unless you are going to go to the source of the information who experienced it directly, then all you are conveying is potentially fact-less, information that won't benefit you or others in the long run. Even when you do relay information heard first hand, what you say would still be your perception and account of the situation.

Gossip can feed negative energy. You can almost feel the surge when it picks up momentum and races off into the distance. Gossip is a hanger on of old, negative energy. The chatting over the garden fence, the twitching of curtains, the incorrect perceptions of everyone else around us, reassuring our old friend the ego. Remember our connection between each other, so gossiping about someone is really gossiping about oneself, and no one likes to be the main subject of gossip.

As you become that little bit more aware and conscious of how you are reacting to a situation, you will find it harder to join in with others and feel uncomfortable. Don't fuel the fire by being part of this formula, try to rise above. Begin to see your world from a higher perspective. Say very little and send out energetically into the Universe love and support to the one being gossiped about and the ones who are doing the gossiping.

The Undercarriage

ANCESTRAL AUTOMATIC TRANSMISSION

"Far reaching rust that invades a car's body can weaken structural elements over time. If rust affects key structural components of a vehicle such as the frame or chassis, it can jeopardize the car's reliability."

Prevention of rust:

"Pain travels through families until someone is ready to feel it, take action and bring it to a complete stop as quickly and as safely as possible." (Stephi Wagner.)

An innovative and forward way of thinking is to consider how the effects of your ancestor's emotional responses to situations, are affecting you now. Just like a car that has sped past and splashed you, the watery residue from the puddle has randomly left negative energy onto your energy field. Some of it will drip off you while the rest may seep into your undercarriage, these are elements of your ancestor's residual energy. This energy has an emotion attached to it that may still be trying to flow freely and has become blocked over time, without an outlet it has transmuted from generation to generation. It could be a response from trauma, low self-worth, low self-belief, ingrained traditional opinions, loss, grief, prejudice, wealth, poverty, status, overall health and temperament.

Of course, without your ancestors, you wouldn't be here. Without your ancestors you wouldn't have been manufactured into the human that you are today. Without your ancestors you would not have had the opportunity to have experienced, experiences.

All those that have existed before you have undergone countless highs, lows and everything in between. From discrimination, suppression, wars, segregation, poverty, abuse, pain, chronic illness, unfinished business and

regret to joyous moments, excitement, wealth, unique abilities, health, freedom, opportunity and motivational moments.
If something within is provoked by an experience that has caused you emotional pain or challenged you and made you feel a deep sense of injustice, unhappiness, shame, guilt or negativity; it's possible that it could be due to the aftereffects of ancestral residual energy entrenching itself inside your vehicle. The complexities of this are profound and you may find it challenging to differentiate between something that is old and surplus, from that which you have always believed to be the truth and belonging to you. Something that although causes great pain, family rifts and hardship, is excused because to discuss would appear weak and open painful, unhealed wounds. Or an attitude of misconstrued acceptance of a behaviour or family trait, creating a sense of betrayal for all those who have suffered before you, etc.
Your Soul is giving you a nudge at this point, especially when it is starting to affect your health and well–being. It's encouraging you to search for the possible causes, to start the process of unblocking and releasing this negativity so that you can prevent the rust from spreading from you to further generations.
Although these ancestors went on to create the forthcoming generations, filtered down to each generation can be the negative responses of old traumas, pain, insecurity and sadness, that did not have an outlet. The residual emotions can flow its way through your lineage to you and your energy field. This is an energy that requires clearing and healing, so you don't have to experience the symptoms of their pain, that wasn't associated with you in the first place, but needs to be freed for your benefit, and future generations to come. By doing this you can become more aware of all the positive elements you have running through your system.
Rather like the corrosion that rust can cause on a vehicle, ancestral low vibrational energy can have the same effect on you. Yet, by understanding that your ancestor's circumstances at the time led them unknowingly to make decisions that took your family down a road of pain, can put an emergency stop on the continuation of suffering from the negative vibration and allow your ancestors to finally rest. You can honour your ancestors by focusing on all the positive elements that you possess, and let the past suffering be set free.
As you start to comprehend this, changing of the energetic frequency to one that is positive, light, and uplifting, allows any of the old rust within to be eradicated. The corrosive nature of rust can cause damage to the look and function of a vehicle. With that in mind, consider any corrosive energy that might be bleeding through your family and its lineage.
We've discussed the effects of stress, anxiety, overwhelm, and frustration

during your lifetime and how to try to prevent this from occurring to the extent that it begins to affect your whole being, and those around you. We have also discussed the elements of family dynamics that you accepted as being the norm, yet may have been extremely traumatic experiences for you. Taking the brave but necessary road of long-term healing, will certainly protect you from further damage.

Healing yourself, starts the process of healing those who surround you. At times you may feel like you are on a solo road trip. Yet, by embarking on this healing journey, you will be the driving force for change. You are at the front of the queue at the traffic lights. As soon as you begin to heal, the traffic jam starts to disperse, and a sweet flow of trouble-free travel will start to begin.

Advisory

- Begin researching your family history and finding out some facts about their lives and experiences. Any family secrets, traumas, sudden deaths etc, that understandably have had an emotional effect on them.
- Ask family members one or two generations above you about what they know about their relations two or three generations above them. Whether there is a common thread of behaviours, opinions or beliefs. By researching potential causes for their behaviours and actions, you can start to understand why they took that particular route on their life journey.
- Research up to seven generations back is recommended as beyond this, the energy has shifted and isn't quite so potent.
- Write letters of gratitude and of appreciation to your ancestors acknowledging why they reacted to situations and dealt with certain experiences the way they did. Having a better understanding of their circumstances and seeing it from a higher perspective will make the process less emotionally challenging, as you can empathise when you have more information.
- Consider trauma counselling, ancestral healing, or psychotherapy to get to the root cause of any issues you have but you feel don't belong to you. Once the old energy of ancestors is released, their energy will settle, and you will not be the blocked energy outlet anymore.
- Honour your ancestors energetically by acknowledging the sacrifices that they have made, the limitations that they had and how you will power onwards pain free, in their name. This could be done by creating a means of remembrance for them, planting and maintaining a rose symbolising your love for them in the garden for example.

Where there's a blame…….

Perhaps you feel that your parents are to blame for the position you are in, in the stream of traffic and that all the onus on your parents is stuck in you and has nowhere to expel. Contemplate freeing this blame energy and giving it a different outlet. As a child you were not equipped with the tools, emotional maturity or awareness that you now have. You may feel that your needs were not met. You may now crave the reassurance, stability, shelter and healthy love, that you feel you missed out on. Learn how to love and parent your inner child in the way that you feel was missing from your childhood. Seek out your trusted, and non-judgemental support system. Your good friends, partner or likeminded Souls, to discuss and research.

Are you now a parent yourself? Consider the tools you have used in bringing up your own child/children. They were probably the same tools your parents passed on to you with a few positive and negative extras along the way. Your parents did exactly the same. By doing this, (which is quite natural by the way), consciously and unconsciously a channel of rust such as negative belief systems, damaging traditions and entrenched opinions may have seeped through for the next generations. The rust, however, can be prevented from fully taking over.

By taking responsibility for your wellbeing, you are not only empowering yourself, but you are also mentoring the Souls who are connected to you. Through you, you are being the advocate for your ancestors and the medicine for future generations to come.

Rather than holding on to the blocked and supressed resentful energy towards them, (which is a negative vibration), respond by accepting your life, your uniqueness and your power. Release by sending them love through focused intention and positive energy. Honour them in thankfulness for giving you the opportunity to experience this life and acknowledge what great teachers they have been, for you to learn from and to evolve.

If, however, there have been experiences that have caused deep penetrating damage, and loss. Incidents that you can't move away from, then put all your energy into researching methods of healing that will work for you and your situation. If the relationship that is causing you distress, is one that is unhealthy and unbalanced. One that makes you feel small, intimidated, threatened, on edge, overwhelmed and detached from yourself and causes your energy to be depleted to such a degree that you are powerlessly spiralling into a depression – no matter who this is, remove them from your carriageway. This isn't drastic, this is your right of way, it is for your overall wellbeing. For your <u>now</u>. It should be your decision to forgive the actions of the person and not the expectations of society or the opinions of others. Working with a holistic healer, and or therapist will guide you in how to free the blocked energy and begin to repair the damage. As the wounds start to heal, your overall perspective of your experiences will start to lose the negative energetic power. You will be able to separate the actions of the troubled Soul from the Soul that was working with the tools that they were given, and thought were the norm. You don't have to carry on the family traditions anymore, but you do need to take on board that it's not a blame game. It's a healing work in progress.

Apply The Handbrake

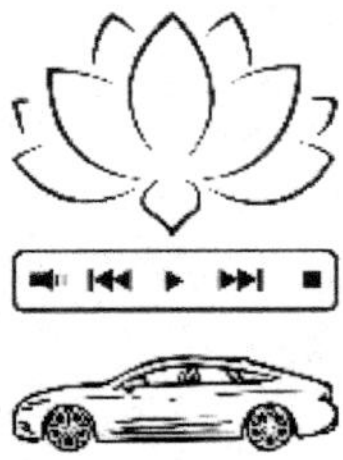

How often do you still your body and mind on a regular basis throughout the day? If you are honest with yourself, it's rare that you probably park up and embrace the quiet opportunity to rest.

Making a conscious decision to slow down, pull over, and apply the handbrake, may be a challenge for you.

When you consider all the activities you experience daily, the different energy vibrations you encounter and unwittingly allow to enter your vehicle, plus all the decisions and choices that you make; all require using substantial amounts of your energy. The level of interaction that you can tolerate when going about your daily life may differ from day-to-day. All the news and social media that can pull you down to a lower vibrational frequency. The unrealistic expectations and the over stimulation of living in current times. Then you can appreciate that finding a parking space to re-set and recharge is going to be extremely beneficial for the upkeep and maintenance of your Soul.

An old, energy draining vibration that you may have experienced, is the belief that to not do anything is being self-indulgent or lazy. With that comes guilt and shame, especially when you are led to believe that you should always have something to show for your day. When someone asks what have you done today, it should not have to make you feel that you need a full-on justification for your actions. Yet it's quite likely that you have been mentored to believe that action means outcome. This belief system has carried on through generation to generation for quite some time now and as you have now realised, has made life's journey that bit harder!

Advisory

Contemplate for a moment how you feel when your day has been hectic, in comparison with when your day was quieter and seemed to flow with ease. When in a state of flow, everything seems less of an effort. It's what you would call a good day. All activities and relations have been favourable, and any changes have helped the cause rather than hindered it. Linear time has slowed, and you've fitted more into the day, at your pace and on your terms. Aim to be less hectic and rushed to experience the many benefits of your journey. Bear in mind that without the challenges, there wouldn't be the motivation to change and improve. The key is to ensure balance, rather than exhaustion and overwhelm taking precedence.

Transport yourself for 5 minutes to regain calm, clarity and confidence
This is a 5-minute parking space practice that you can use anytime, anywhere to regain calm, clarity and confidence. Remember to quite literally park up – <u>Do not do this when driving</u>.

To begin, become physically still, wherever you are, either lying, sitting or standing.

Choose a posture where you'll be as comfortable as possible and lightly close your eyes.

Bring your awareness to whatever is going on for you right now.

Give the weight of your body up to gravity.

Allow the weight to sink into the points of contact between your body and the floor, the chair or bed.

What sensations are there right now?

If you notice any tension or resistance towards painful, unpleasant sensations, gently turn towards them.

Accept them as best you can.

If you begin to tense around the breath, then let go a little bit more each outbreath.

Soften into gravity.

Notice any thoughts as they arise and pass through the mind.

See if you can let them come and go without being able to identify them with their content.

Observe them as if they were clouds in the sky.

Notice any feelings and emotions as they arise.

Can you let them come and go?

Include everything within your awareness with a kindly perspective.

Now, allow your awareness inside the breath, and feel the different sensations in the front, back and sides of the torso.

Can you feel your awareness within the flow of movement of the breath?

Use the breath to anchor your awareness in the present moment breathing in the body, noticing each inhale and exhale again and again.

Each time you notice that your mind has wandered, gently guide it back to the breath deep in the body.

Now, gently expand your awareness to include the whole body.

Feel the weight and shape of the body as it sits, stands or lies.

If you've got any pain or discomfort, make sure your awareness remains open.

Cultivate acceptance or acknowledgement for all of your experiences.

Befriend it.

Use the breath to anchor your awareness in the present moment, breathing in the body, noticing each inhale and exhale again and again.

Now slowly open your eyes and bring your attention back into the room and notice how you feel….and notice what's changed from before you began to do this exercise to now.

You may feel a little bit calmer. Your heart rate may feel a little slower. You may be seeing the room around you with a little bit more clarity.

Maybe your shoulders are more relaxed.

See if you can bring this same quality of kind awareness of soft relaxation in the core of your body and being, with you throughout the day.

Thank you for your mindfulness practice as you continue to feel less and less anxious in your body and mind.

Roadside Assistance

Your Soul is here on earth on a hire purchase. Residing in your vehicle for the period of time your Soul has agreed to. There has been a finance plan already set up and as soon as your Soul enters the world as a human being, your Soul is fulfilling its contract. It may be a short loan, depending on a number of factors or it could be a longer lease. The main thing is that your Soul has come here to learn, experience and evolve. To be a source of knowledge for you and others to learn from. To be the full beam of love, for those whose headlights have dimmed. For your Soul to complete actions that haven't yet been completed and for your Soul to steer towards opportunity and development. Your pitstop team consists of all the loved ones that have passed before you, your ancestors, your angels and your spirit guides. As you take on board the advisories presented, and the layers upon your courtesy light start to lift, you will find that your team can be radioed in and communicated with, in a less static way and on a more clear and uninterrupted energy frequency. All play roles allowing your journey here on earth to be a place of growth and one that fulfils your existence, while in your human form. They're like the ultimate one pit crew. There to be called upon, when necessary, there to protect and ensure your journey on earth goes along the route it signed the paperwork for. Ensuring that all you experience along the way creates an opportunity for your Soul to gather as much experience and growth as it possibly can do. Your Soul has signed the lease contract for your current lifetime. Think of it as if you've read all the small print, the terms and conditions, and signed your name in acceptance, yet for your engine control unit to be survivable here in this existence, you've agreed to a verbal contract as well. You know deep down you accepted and agreed to this, but it's their word against yours. That encapsulates your journey here. It will follow in the direction it is meant to, and you will experience living in the human form.

Think of the team as your inner navigation system providing you with the best route your Soul needs to take to reach the arranged destination, yet allowing you to have free-will, to choose and decide your preferred method of arrival. The destination never changes, the routes may vary but eventually all roads will align. Your Soul will upgrade when its journey of education and development is finally completed. Your Soul is extremely curious though, and what may seem like a lifetime is but a flash of the headlights in terms of time, so your Soul is on a road of endless discovery. As one journey comes to an end another will begin. Earth is a fast-track way of feeding your Soul's intrigue, so it may choose to return for a few more goes for good measure or decide on another destination or even a different form of existence altogether.

Your Soul is LOVE. Behind the scenes, your pitstop crew are forever loving you and emanating Love and are encouraging you to embrace all experiences with love and light energy.

Because of the interconnectedness of us all, we are all providing a service for all other Souls too. You have no overall control about what occurs because it was meant to be. It was meant to go the way that it has so far, for the effects, teachings and lessons of yourself and others. You, me and we are all part of this huge yet short road trip on earth.

The courtesy light that we have discussed, is your inner love and energetic life force that is connected to a higher power radiating from within and out to all those around you on a Soul level.

Never feel that you are alone on this unique journey. In the hard and challenging times your pit crew are there within, and around you and backing you all the way, and they are with you for the joy, happiness and fun, they are just on a different realm of existence.

Your pit crew are waiting in the pit box, there if you radio in for assistance, and when you need to take a pit stop, this highly coordinated team will work with their precision and speed to ensure you are safely on your way, trouble-free.

Advisory

Take a deep breath, apply the handbrake and let what has been said, take a moment to sink in. The words you have read are powerful and you may feel a little emotional. As if a sweet breeze of realisation has come over you. A feeling of "Coming home". This is normal and beautiful. That's your pitstop team giving you a little nudge.

To know you have this back up team, may take a little time to adjust to. If you've never contemplated that you are supported on a Soul level before, it might be a difficult concept for you to consider. You may have been driving along quite happily and then a sudden swerve is required as an obstruction in the road causes you to go off course and this may make you sense that you need more support and guidance along the way. It could be that you have felt like this for some time, and this helpful little guidebook has landed on your passenger seat, just at the right time!

Without being consciously aware, your pitstop team have been supporting your Soul throughout the highs and lows. Encouraging you to embrace your human life with a fully fuelled Soul instead of a half tank, half-awake human doing way of being.

Your pitstop team are subtle. They won't necessarily grab the steering wheel suddenly and drive you off course, but they will grab the steering wheel to guide you back on the right road. They will begin to flash up some Belisha beacon moments which could intensify if you choose not to listen to the messages. These could be repeating situations and circumstances, or repeated thoughts and an intuitive pull towards deciding. For example, your car insurance needs renewing, and you put it off. Over the course of the days and weeks prior to looking at some quotes, you see or hear adverts for insurance options and companies on a regular basis, or you are aware of someone having to make an insurance claim, when normally you wouldn't really think about it. Your pitstop team are there for the minor as well as the major decisions that crop up along the way.

The more you begin to accept their existence the more supported you will feel when the more challenging experiences occur. As you head along your awakening journey you are beginning to sense things on a different level, and communication with your pit stop team will become that bit easier as the layers thin and are removed.

To begin a more open, two-way relationship with your pitstop team could be something as simple as you requesting a recognisable sign that they are with you. This will be personal to you. Try not to put any time frame restrictions on their response. When they answer your call, it will be subtle and not necessarily when you expect it to be, yet be open to anything that appears to be in sync with your request.

Often, when under duress, scared or having difficulties, you may have been drawn to something within. You may have quietly requested support from someone or something. You may wonder why you were pulled to ask for assistance to such a degree, but that is your Soul radioing in to your pitstop team for them to leap into action.

You are here to experience life on earth and as an energy you have tuned into the overall conscious energy frequency that has been heavy and limiting. You are now at the starting grid of being able to call back your power and being more conscious of your pitstop team's support and assistance than you perhaps were ever aware of before. You will experience symbolic messages in your dreams, information that feels intuitive – known as downloads – where you have a strong desire or pull towards something that is beneficial to you or others. Synchronicities that are personalised to you, reinforcing their presence. Each member of your crew has a specific role and will work tirelessly as a team to ensure you remain in pole position.

By tuning in you may notice subtle coincidences that are aligned with you. Such as regularly hearing the same song on the radio. Often this is your pitstop team informing you they are around you, supporting you at this time and that you are on the right road. They will connect with you through the lyrics of that specific song.

Have you ever properly listened to the words of certain songs, or just let the music wash over you? Words in songs are often little messages that align with you at that current time. Above anything else it's quite interesting to fathom out what the message might be. What might be an annoying ear worm at the time might be a message of love and support if you only listened to the lyrics. You may feel a physical sensation such as a light breeze or a fragrance smell that you associate with a loved one, indicating that they are close by. You may see numbers on clocks, tills or even the washing machine align. 11.11 or 22.22 for example. Or a Robin may follow you on a walk, flying quite close by and chirruping happily. You may be inexplicably delayed setting off for somewhere, this being purposefully orchestrated, so you are kept safe. These are all examples of the subtle means of communicating their love, guidance and support.

Your pitstop team are under strict instructions that you have free will and that ultimately you have the choice to make your own decisions. You might be frustrated with that concept. That if they are here to support and guide you, then they should tell you what to do and how to do it, yet they allow you to go on a totally alternative route. This is where you may get confused and feel unsupported. Everything is divinely planned and timed for your greater good however, so even if you take the long way round, your support team, though on a slightly different realm, are still guiding, loving and supporting you. Just allow the flow of energy to freely move and like a traffic policeman; point you in the direction that you eventually need to take.

DIAGNOSTIC SOUL SURVEY (PART 2)

Right at the start of the manual you were asked to complete your Soul Diagnostic Survey. Let's see if there has been any energetic shifts, changes or improvements along the way.

DIAGNOSTIC SYMPTOMS

1-4 score

POWER LOSS
Lethargic, tired, feeling flat/low.

VIBRATIONS
Get upset easily, feel panicky, physical symptoms, such as lack of sleep.

OVER-HEATING
Regularly losing your temper, snappy, lack of control.

DIFFICULTY STARTING
Your get up and go has got up and gone.

SLOW ACCELERATION
Lack of motivation, sluggish, short bursts of energy but not sustained.

BRAKES BEHAVING DIFFERENTLY
Procrastinating, uninterested in tasks or activities.

NOISE
Sensitive to noise, overstimulated and overwhelmed in busy places.

SUDDEN ENGINE FAILURE DUE TO WRONG FUEL
I have nightmare/terrors. I suffer with indigestion and stomach aches.

GOOD RUNNING ORDER
Overall, you feel like everything is ok.

FREE OF MECHANICAL PROBLEMS
Calm, grounded and even tempered.

IDLES SMOOTHLY
I can sit still easily and am calm. I'm patient and tolerant. I can breathe in and out easily.

NOT MOVING
Sleeping well with no interruptions.
No feelings of guilt, remorse or regret.

NONE OR A LITTLE	SOME OF THE TIME	A GOOD PART OF THE TIME	MOST OF THE TIME
1	2	3	4

The Higher Power Source

Throughout this book, you have been guided and advised in certain practices that enables your Soul, body and mind to be maintained in a healthy, balanced way and ensures that your human experience is as bountiful and trouble free as it possibly can be. It has explained the various routes that you have unwittingly taken and demonstrated that there are alternative roads out there, that will enhance your overall experience and has provided you with information that you may not have even contemplated before, yet as you read on you perhaps felt comforted, safe and understood. All this has come from a higher source of power, through me to you, and on to these pages.

So, what is the Higher-Power Source? It is the source of energy that is so intrinsically connected to your Soul, and to other Souls. The energy that is nothing and is everything. Energy that drives through all that exists. That which governs how energy and matter interact and shape your physical and mental experiences. The energy that is the highest of frequencies, one of high vibrational, love and power.

The car battery that creates energy to start your engine, powers up all your components and keeps your engine running. A source of great mystery yet familiarity. A source of wonder and intrigue, questions and answers. A source of feast and famine, dark and light, wisdom and strength. The source of all knowledge, honour and order. The Higher Power energy that can be accessed and directed. That which can transfer power with the potential for depletion or renewal. The power of source that can be transferred through intention and mindful practice, yet can deplete through negativity, stress and long-term lack of replenishment. The energy that is intangible and boundless.

By travelling on my own journey of awakening, I have practiced and developed a communication with not only my pit stop team of guides, angels, loved ones and ancestors - but through them, via my Soul, I have accessed messages from the higher source of power. One of them being a rather strong push to encourage me to write the book you have been reading! By being in tune with a higher frequency this is easier than it once was, and as my Soul has grown and evolved, I feel I am where I should be at this current time. However, my journey continues, and even if you are at the very beginning of your own journey of awakening, I hope you can take some, if not all of the contents of this book along with you on your road trip and reconnect with the wisdom that is inside of us all.

Advisory

Imagine that you are the jump start leads, and that the world is charged by the car battery. Using your high vibrational energy, the battery can be continuously recharged as you begin the journey of feeding what your Soul is gently requesting, love, light, peace, abundance, acceptance, serenity, strength, bliss, compassion and joy. As you gradually feel at one within and hold the space of trust and peace, your energetic vibration changes too and that then flows out to the big battery.

If you concentrate on your little corner of the world, (your reality) and you ensure that you are regularly "checking in" on the maintenance of your Soul and boosting your energy levels regularly, prioritising your needs and requirements and considering how you react and respond to situations, you then energetically send a high vibrational, healing frequency out into the wider world. Out to the collective, out to the battery. The world will hold your light, and powerful, positive energy and spread throughout the world, powering on.

Hidden Extras!!

The Small Print

- Trust your intuition. Move beyond the limitations you put upon yourself
- Devote your time to tune in to your heart. What advice does it give you today?
- Your beauty goes beyond your looks and bodywork. Overcome any negative traits in your thoughts and choices.
- There are wonderous and miraculous changes occurring. Remember your thoughts are magnetic and very powerful.
- You are in the precious keeping of love and light. Don't be fooled that you are alone and separate. We are all connected.
- You may feel overwhelmed and tired with the state of affairs now. The only way to heal the world right now is to first heal ourselves.
- Take a moment to step back and let things develop naturally. Reassess the situation in your heart before proceeding any further.
- Don't be afraid to share your gifts. Allow the wave of inspiration to journey into the lives of others.
- Gossip, judgement and criticism carry low energetic vibrational frequencies. Practice compassion, understanding and patience to raise the vibration.
- There is much going on underneath the surface. Know that the subtle realm is gently guiding you onwards and upwards.
- If you've made a mistake, caused upset or used hurtful words, OWN IT.
- Don't make excuses. Accept and apologise with sincerity. Observe how quickly the energy lifts.
- What a gift you are! Think of all those who would miss you if you weren't in their lives anymore. Never forget the positive effect you have on all those around you. YOU matter.
- Imagine your thankyou speech at an awards ceremony. Who would you thank first and why? How can you show your gratitude to those who are important to you?

- Trust in the unknown. There's so much we cannot explain but do we really have to? Welcome the unexplained and embrace your curiosity.
- Be fearless and stand strong. Embrace your inner Bentley. Be devoted and committed to your cause.
- Relight the fire within. Don't allow it to be extinguished during difficult times. Keep burning on, and when you begin to smoulder, rekindle the embers.
- As you gradually heal, you won't be immune to having some bad days along the way. You will have the tools to navigate through though, so don't give up on you.
- Your version of your life is exactly that. Your version. Others will have similar experiences but never quite the same as what you have encountered. That's what makes you unique.
- Think of your Soul as the supplement magazine in a Sunday paper. Once you've gone beyond the glossy photos, you'll discover some deep and meaningful articles within.
- Don't forget that this is your journey. It may seem that what you do or say is odd or different to some, yet if it is your true and authentic self, it's no one else's business!
- Give yourself permission to enjoy success and happiness. You should experience the joy of satisfaction, reward and fulfilment. It isn't wrong to go for gold!
- All the hard work while working on yourself is a fantastic gift to give your future self who will be forever grateful for your efforts. Don't give up on yourself. The rewards await to be reaped.
- The choices you make define you much more than your circumstances ever will.
- Happiness is a journey, not a destination. Enjoy living in the moment and embracing all the moments of joy.
- The past can't be changed. Yet how you deal with the present is ever moving. Any residual energy left over from moments of the past, can be released and forgiven. Learn and move on.
- You're not stuck. You are just resting and giving your energy the time to align and settle where it should, before giving you another burst of inspiration.

- We can try to drive in the cars of others and be as empathic as possible, but we will never truly know how another Soul really is feeling. With this in mind, consider what goes on behind closed doors, and just be kind.
- Some days you feel like you're the juggler and the clown. The lion tamer and the plate spinner. Life can be a circus sometimes and quite the balancing act. For today, be the ringmaster.
- Although we are all connected, we are all unique and individual. Some you meet will be on your wavelength, some won't and that's okay. It's nothing personal; it's a vibrational difference.
- Consider bumping into your future self. What might surprise you in your conversation and inspire you for the coming months and years ahead?
- We may be unaware that we are carrying the energy of others. If it's negative, draining energy, this will cause issues. Take time to discover whether what you carry is yours, and if not; release it with love.
- Worry less and smile more. Laugh and love. Sometimes life can be intense and challenging. It's how we respond during the harder times that will speed up the arrival of better times.
- Rest easy. The best medicine to heal, both physically and emotionally is good quality sleep. Sign off from the phone and have an uninterrupted kip, for your overall good health and wellbeing.
- Treat today as a day of firsts. Look at the sky as if for the first time, a tree, a flower, a bee, a bubble or even yourself. Focus on the magic of seeing whatever you choose as if for the first time.
- Try not to judge yourself too harshly. Life doesn't come with an instruction manual – other than this one of course!
- Unlike a new car, your Soul doesn't depreciate in value. You are priceless and with age comes wisdom and experience. Remember you're unique and you run on your energy. No one else can drive your car the way you handle yours.

This is not the end of your journey. It is merely the start. I've handed over to you some of the tools that will set you up sufficiently to continue on your personal road trip. Weaving in and out of this guidebook, I have permeated the pages with high vibrational, potent energy.
As I wave you off on what might be the toughest but most beautiful trips of your life; please make sure that your oil is topped up, your water squirter reservoir is overflowing, your tyres are at the correct pressure and your fuel tank is full!

Connecting Rods

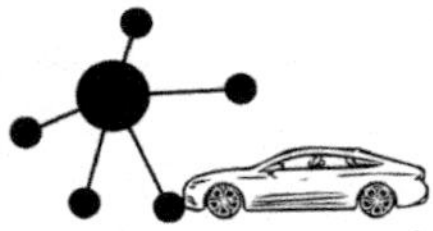

Here are some useful methods of healing to keep that vibe nice and high!

- NHS referral.
- Employment and education facilities.
- National Hypnotherapy Society – Lists private hypnotherapists local to you.
- National Counselling Society – Lists private counsellors and psychotherapists local to you.
- psychologytoday.com – Psychology Today is a website and magazine that is dedicated to publishing content about human behaviour and mental health written by experts in the field. It also lists local private therapists.
- Holistic Therapists: Search for specific modalities, here's a list of therapeutic options: Acupuncture, Acupressure, Ancestral Healing, Angel Healing, Aromatherapy, Breathwork, Coaching, Crystal Healing, Sound therapy, Spiritual Hypnotherapy/counselling, Massage, Meditation, Mindfulness, Reflexology, Reiki, Yoga.

About Me

Rachel is a qualified hypnotherapist, psychotherapist, healer and intuitive. She is a mother, partner and cat parent, practicing in the picturesque New Mill just outside Holmfirth.
Still experiencing her own spiritual awakening, her inspiration for this book was to ensure that anyone else embarking on their own journey of evolution, would have a go – to guidebook.
One that would support, encourage and guide you through what can be a tough, challenging and at times lonely road trip.

Notes and Observations

Printed in Dunstable, United Kingdom

74805154R00077